The Will to Live Project

REBECCA WILD

Copyright © 2024 Rebecca Wild

All rights reserved.

ISBN: 9798870185200

DEDICATION

With the burning faith that this is only my first book, and that you'll all get your chance, this book is dedicated to the woman who inspired me to write. To the woman who showed me that beauty and magic truly is everywhere if you look hard enough. And to the woman whose words have saved me more times than I can count.

Elizabeth Gilbert, you changed my life.

CONTENTS

Authors Note	i
Part 1: EXISTENCE	1
Lesson 1: Initiation	7
Lesson 2: Seek Peace Over Happiness	12
Lesson 3: Crack Right Open	16
Lesson 4: The Only Way Out is Through	20
Lesson 5: (You're Not Special, It's Not Personal, There's No One Coming to Save You)	25
Lesson 6: What If Your Purpose Isn't Accolades?	28
Lesson 7: You Are Already Changing the World	31
Part 2: OTHERS	35
Lesson 8: If You're Not Full of Yourself, What Are You Full Of?	40
Lesson 9: But Culture Makes It So	44
Lesson 10: It's Not Me, It's You. It's Not You, It's Me	48
Lesson 11: We Were All Children Once	52
Lesson 12: I'm Not Intimidating, You're Intimidated	56
Lesson 13: No One Owes You Airtime	59
Lesson 14: How It Made You Feel Doesn't Mean It Is the Truth	62
Part 3: LOSS AND CRISIS	65

Lesson 15: For Five Minutes	70
Lesson 16: Death Is for The Living	73
Lesson 17: Regulation Station	77
Lesson 18: To Love and Let Go	83
Lesson 19: You Are So Much More Than How You Think About Yourself When You're Afraid	86
Lesson 20: You'll Find the Chaos If That's What You Believe In	90
Part 4: DATING YOURSELF	**94**
Lesson 21: The Little Ways You Love Yourself	100
Lesson 22: The Getting to Know Yourself List	104
Lesson 23: Another You in The Room	108
Lesson 24: Storytelling Love into Existence	111
Lesson 25: Inner Polarity	114
Lesson 26: Get Into Your Body	118
Part 5: RELATIONSHIPS	**123**
Lesson 27: The Science of Love	130
Lesson 28: I Don't Want to Be Your Everything	134
Lesson 29: Self-Abandonment and Breaking Out	138
Lesson 30: Rising In Love	142
Lesson 31: Basic Human Needs	148
Lesson 32: The Little Affirmations of Love List	152
Lesson 33: What's Your Role?	156

Part 6: HABITS	160
Lesson 34: Laziness is a Myth	164
Lesson 35: There Are No Coincidences	167
Lesson 36: Energy Rituals	171
Lesson 37: If It's Meant to Be in Your Life, It Will Be	173
Lesson 38: Let's All Cry About It	177
Lesson 39: The Opposite of Trauma Is Play (and other useful life tips)	180

AUTHORS NOTE

WARNING:

This book will offend you. In fact, I hope that it does. I hope that it fills you with more questions than answers, has you scribbling in a notebook at 2am in your parents' house as you fish through ancient pieces of your life in the hunt for clues. I hope that it makes you desperately uncomfortable and equally fills you with a yearning you've never known before. I hope that it makes you so curious about yourself that you become Detective Inspector of Your Soul.

You are reading the collated words of a sometimes un-intentionally preachy and arrogant twenty-something white female. There is lots I won't get right. This whole book has been spellchecked and formatted by my own tired and impatient eyes. There will be lots I have got wrong. But please know that this book comes from an intense desire to heal. I want life to be easier for you. I want you to recognise how wonderful you are without anyone else telling you first. I want you to have chances and opportunities, because you won't be the one holding yourself back anymore.

There might be things you disagree with, and that's okay. Take what resonates and leave the rest. Stay curious. Stay learning. Stay open-minded to your own changes. I'm right in that boat with you too.

I hope that this book offends you.

LYL.

PART 1: EXISTENCE

Most authors of self-help books open by telling you about the 'grand revelation' that made them begin their 'fixing themselves' journey. It's usually along the lines of 'I heard a voice as I was crying on the floor in the darkness' or a humbling tale of someone who had it worse than them, helping them see the light.

But that's just poetic narrative.

You see, hitting rock bottom isn't always what it looks like in the movies. No crying on the staircase, clinging on to the photo of the parent/loved one/pet that was no longer there, no line of cocaine on a bloodstained bathroom floor in the house of someone you don't know the name of, no-for me, it was an 11pm Monday night trip to Morrison's.

I switched the engine on in my car and set a playlist for the two-minute trip to the supermarket, turning my speakers up full and inching my window down slightly so that everyone could hear. Glancing at the clock on my dashboard it said 10:52, meaning I had eight minutes left - that was - if I really wanted to do this, before they closed. "Yep" I said out loud and sped off down my road.

I can't quite explain how I was feeling that night. I'd been on antidepressants for around three months at this point, and for those of you who don't know antidepressants, there is no other way than to say that they literally took away all my feelings. No sadness, no grief, no anger, obviously no happy thoughts, but underlying it all lay a sense of discomfort. Something wasn't quite right. I mean duh, I was on antidepressants, but it was more than that. It was as if my real non-drugged-up self was calling through the echoing prison cell walls I had encased it in to stop the negative feelings, and was telling me to let it go, to let it be free. Of course, under no circumstances did I feel like I was quite ready for that, so I guess this phase was kind of... a detour.

The shop was quiet, I mean it would be, it was nearly eleven on a Monday night and half of my aging town went to sleep three hours ago. I'm sure a determined-looking teenager storming to the back of the shop wasn't a reassuring sight for anyone there who was hoping to get off on time that night. But at last, I had made it: "Hair Dye".

OKAY, OKAY, slightly dramatic I know, but this was a major deal for me. For the last eighteen years of my life, I'd been brought up believing that hair dye, nail polish, ear piercings and make-up were 'bad things' for 'bad people'. So, buying hair dye - to me - was the equivalent of purchasing a one-way ticket to hell and chucking the receipt.

To most people I'm sure that changing the colour of your hair is a simple 'Oh, I wonder if brown would suit me?' or 'Heather's sister has red hair, maybe I should try it?' but for me, I was making a point. Like a full on 'I'm-a-slightly-messed-up-teenager-and-no-one-can-stop-me' kind of point. And walking into sixth form the next day definitely created the effect that I wanted. The glares and whispers and 'what the hell have you done!'s only satisfied my twisted ego more, and I sapped it all up like a bee to nectar. This was the beginning of the rest of my life, and I couldn't wait.

*

Seven years and many more late-night bathroom box dyes later had passed, and I was yet again staring helplessly at myself in the mirror waiting for my hair to develop and fix all my problems. I was taking it back to brunette. My roots. The 'real me'. Trying to reclaim the parts of myself I had neglected for so long. Trying to remember where my courage and bravery had gone. Trying.

How was I back here? Had I gone anywhere at all? I had nothing to say for it other than an empty savings account and slightly more defined cheekbones where anxiety had eaten my baby fat away. Life was heavier than ever, and equally as uneventful. The world felt muggy, the air thick with pessimism and fear. Being a human felt exhausting and I really didn't have the energy for it anymore.

I was angry, furious in fact. This wasn't how my life was supposed to be. I was supposed to be so much more than this. Bigger, better, more polished. And instead, my fragile mental health and the autoimmune diseases that followed meant I couldn't hold a job down for longer than nine months. Other people were growing an entire lifeform in that time, whilst I was spending most of it figuring out how to quit. I had, on all accounts of everything I had learnt about 'what I was supposed to be', failed.

"It doesn't have to be this hard" The Doctor said. What on earth could she mean? Had she seen the absolute car crash that my life had become? I was in my mid-twenties feeling like I'd experienced several lifetimes of trauma in one. I was moving back in with my parents with no money or prospects. I made Winnie the Pooh look like more of an adult than I was. "You don't have to keep suffering like this" she continued, and added sedatives to my already long list of prescription meds. My bathroom looked like a pharmacy at this point, but hey, I was a sucker for Western pharmaceuticals. And the medicines I had to take because of the side effects of the other medicines I was on had meant my collection had now burst out into the bedroom drawers too. We were one big dysfunctional family, and they gave me a delightful false sense of control that I so desperately desired.

But I'm missing a major part of my story. And maybe this is where it all went wrong. From early childhood, me and Big T traumas had gotten to know each other well. From childhood sexual abuse, natural disasters, rape, neglect, pregnancy loss, domestic violence and grief, by early adulthood I was exhausted. And I would've been forgiven had I told you then that I had no hope left and wanted to give up. Everyone would have understood.

But that wasn't what happened.

In 2020, the year the world stopped, I dealt with two major breakups, job loss and serious health scares, and also had the best year of my life. *That's* the problem.

I became this glowing piece of sunshine, radiating joy everywhere to everyone. I had joy to give away. I woke up every day feeling like I was in a movie and went to bed every night in fits of giggles as I told each piece of furniture in my house to 'sleep well'. I created life changing online content that millions of people were uplifted by. I made a podcast and learnt to date myself for the very first time. I danced naked under the stars and ran barefoot through woodlands singing at the top of my voice. Every day I woke up feeling ALIVE.

And now? I don't.

Had I not known life could feel like that (for a whole year) then maybe I would be okay. Maybe it's the yearning that's broken my spirit, maybe it's just knowing that that was all possible for me. That in that duration of my life where I took hardships as lessons and accepted all of my feelings with compassion and movement, life felt easy. All those horrendous traumas felt worth it. I recognised then that they had made me who I am today. I never thought any of that would be possible for me.

Somewhere in the moments that ended that year I entered a new phase. A painful, immersive, dark one. One that has worn me down so much that although I don't want to die, I'm not really that bothered about being here either[i]. I've forgotten what joy feels like. I'm filled with bitterness and resent. I am the Scrooge of all things good in the world.

And to me, it feels like the greatest unsolved missing persons mystery of all time. Where did I go?

I felt like the grown-ups at the end of Polar Express who couldn't hear the sound of Santas sleigh bell anymore. I looked around at the British Springtime unfurling rapidly around me and felt nothing. I could see the luscious rich green of the new grass sprouting up in every corner. I could see the blues and yellows and pinks of bluebells and daffodils and tulips. I watched precious day-old lambs take their first few steps on solid ground. And I felt nothing. I was seeing in colour but feeling in dull greys. Was it depression, or was I just tired? Did I just know too much? Had I just experienced too much pain to see it any other way now? Maybe I just finally saw that the world and culture we are living in is not designed for humans to thrive?

For a long time I thought I needed to be 'fixed' and 'perfect' to write this book. 2020 me, as I called her. But then I realised that actually, the only way to write this book was broken, and hurting, and knowing pain like this, and feeling darkness the way I do. It was the only way all the things I needed to say would be said. Self-help isn't designed to fix you. That's what *you* are for. But it is designed to help show you different ways of doing the hard stuff. Better ways to manage it.

Sometimes.

I have always been the detective of my soul, human existence, happiness and emotion. In the desperation and longing to understand where I had lost myself, I began a quest: The Will to Live Project. I decided to journey back in a mission to find my missing pieces, and along the way share with you the lessons that have been pivotal in surviving the impossible.

And hopefully, along the way, find The Will to Live too.

LYL.

LESSON 1: INITIATION

Welcome to hell.

Wait, no one told you? Damn.

Guess that's my job then.

I, like many of you, came here oblivious. Blindsided. Naïve. I assumed it was my right to have everything the folks in the movies had. The fairy-tale romance. The white picket fences. The perfect children, the raging social life, the great career, all the money I could ever need.

I also assumed that that was what I wanted.

I assumed, if I had it all, everyone would like me.

I assumed, that if everyone liked me, life would be easy.

And then you reach adulthood. You even get some of those things. Sometimes all of those things.

And it's still shit.

And thus begins the quest. "It must be me!" you cry. "Maybe I'm broken!". (You're getting warmer).

You begin your 'healing journey'. Your 'wellness path'. You start drinking celery juice and snorting sage. You buy all the books and courses and 'containers'. You outgrow friendships and evaluate the relationships with your family. You show your tits to the full moon once a month and keep crystals in your knicker draw to repel fuckboys and thrush.

Sometimes it works. You feel like you're getting closer. Maybe you are?

But it's deeper than that. It's core-deep, no-amount-of-therapy-will-make-me-happy-here deeper. It's deeper than depression and anxiety and whatever labels the doctors on TikTok give you that make you feel safer.

It all went wrong when we assumed this was meant to be a good time.

We all have different projections and concepts around the meaning of existence. Oftentimes they give us a sense of relief. It's nice to feel that we're not just random cells thrown about in random places. I think it's important actually. My meaning of existence (which I'm boldly about to share with you, it is my book after all), just pisses me off a bit.

This is my souls last life on earth. My soul has been here since the beginning, and remembers many of the experiences I have had, places I have lived, roles I have partaken in. I have been an English queen, swashbuckling pirate, snobby ancient Egyptian royalty and even a coked-up prostitute across my times on earth.

It's been a blast, truly.

It is my belief that once our bodies die, our souls go back up to a pretty awesome place where it is easy and fun and joyful and just generally great. You get to reunite with your soul family, the team who has been there with you through all of your journeys on earth (either as fellow humans, animals or spirit guides) and you reflect on what went well and what could've gone better. You hear phrases like 'ah, better luck next time buddy!' and 'you'll get it soon, I'm sure!'.

Because it's really fucking hard to get it. All the learning. That's why we come down here you see, to get a 'FastTrack' at learning emotions and peace and love and all that jazz. We could've stayed up there, in that super comfy place with happiness and joy and no suffering. But the learning process is slow and not as immersive.

We are the brave ones, for choosing to come here, to hell.

So, here's how it went at the bitter end of my last life (the coked-up prostitute being reintegrated into the modern world after quite a long gap between lives and time periods): I said something along the lines of 'ah fuck it, go on then, one more go'.

Sighs.

And wait, here's the best part: *you* get to design the things that fuck you up here. Like a play. You get to choose how to ruin your own life. Isn't that neat? There's a big meeting where you write the story, and ask yourself (and this is important): "What could I do to me that would really break me and ensue a huge healing and learning experience that will catapult my evolutional learning and growth? Oh, and probably not kill me in the process?"

So, welcome to hell, you created it.

And this is the part I get pissed off at. My character, my personality, is a go-getter. An, 'I won't stop can't stop' kinda chic. An, 'I can do anything even if I can't' kinda gal. This is problematic for me because on designing my play of this lifetime, several of my trusted advisors said things along the lines of 'Are you sure?' and 'This might be a bit much?'.

And what did I say?

"Fuck it."

It's reassuring to me that I curated the carnage and the suffering for myself, it's kind of cute. Particularly when I'm at rock bottom, and the most unhinged and bizarre tornado of a life event occurs. Reminding myself that I chose it because I specifically knew it would destroy me (in order to rebuild myself) genuinely does help.

What did I say about meaning of existence providing us with relief, eh?

Making meaning of being here helps. We are, after all, in the end times, and it can be terribly hard to see meaning when we are flooded with darkness from every angle of this earth. Or at least, that's what we'll have ourselves believe...

Having had the pleasure of helping other people explore their past lives too, it's clear that our souls often carry core wounding that goes far beyond the damage and psychology of this lifetime and instead resonates deeply inside the essence of our souls. Our conscious minds don't get given that information for free though, which is why I am actually a fan of the new age spirituality 'feel your feelings' era (but also: excessive use of new age spirituality may be harmful to health, please participate responsibly).

'The Awakening', 'The Age of Aquarius', or whatever you would like to call this era, has given us a free pass at skipping the past-life-insomnia issue. We are beginning to remember. Not entirely, otherwise we'd all be living in communes and talking to trees by now, but partly.

Let me explain.

It was good old Carl Jung that first coined the concept of the collective unconscious[ii], the mysterious concept that we're all connected to something bigger than us that provides us with knowledge, insights, wisdom, predisposed fears and behaviours, and more. The Chinese call it Qi, (pronounced 'chi') and believe that Qi energy imbalance creates dis-ease[iii], which can be realigned through meditative techniques, breathwork, rituals, acupuncture, reiki and more. Christians call it God. Spirituality gurus call it 'The Universe'. And the stoners call it pot.

I connect to the Chakras concept too – and imagine the spine as a sort of 'transmitter aerial' to the 'pretty awesome place' I referred to earlier. Through this we can receive messages and insights from within ourselves and through the collective (I, like a true new ager, refer to it as 'Spirit'). Memories and learnings from our past lives can come through here too. Either on our own accord, or with the help of techniques like hypnosis and meditation. I truly believe in the saying 'you already know what you need to do', because I think you do have the answers should you be able to access them. And that's the catch.

This fancy sounding aerial we've acquired can get blocked up pretty easily. And this is where your external situations *and* being in a human body play the part. Our energy channels can get blocked up from internal imbalance; our emotional and physical challenges in this life, the toxins in the air and in our food, water and clothes, destructive behaviour patterns and general emotional disconnect. These are just some of the ways internal harmony and connection to 'self and spirit' - aka, aerial thingy - can be disrupted. The further we get from optimal physical human experience, the further we are from accessing and freeing up those channels. Excitingly, new age spirituality has caught on (honestly, it was about time), and if you're still reading this, then it looks like you have too.

So, it's good news. We're late to the party but the DJ's not leaving yet. Because here's the thing about hell – they never said we couldn't throw a Rager[iv] whilst we were here.

LESSON 2: SEEK PEACE OVER HAPPINESS

Once you begin to see all the painful, impossible, infuriating challenges as clues, lessons and guides that you have curated for your own benefit, it all becomes a bit of a joke really. And once you begin to see that impermanence is okay, that we all get back together again after our human body dies anyway, then it all gets a lot less serious.

You stop cutting the fat off the bacon. You stop saving the nice dress for the special occasion and just wear it every damn day instead. You embrace death and life with equal feeling. With this mindset you can *experience* life here, not just survive it.

But there's a lot of practice and unlearning to be done to be able to achieve that. We are far too attached to the things that make us feel safe for it to be easy to feel happy all the time, if at all. Survival mode has been such a commonplace mindset for so many for so long that it's no wonder it's hard to give it up when we no longer need it anymore. In fact, striving for happiness is how we ended up in this mess anyway, isn't it?

See, here's the thing about happiness. It is seen, worldwide, as the epitome of emotional success. We feed off feeds that show joy and light and laughter. Smiling faces draw us in like kids to a candy shop. It's what we must want. It's what everyone wants. It IS life, right? And it's no surprise we crave it, studies have shown that being 'happy' makes us live longer[v],[vi] puts us at lower risk for heart disease and infection[vii], helps us eat healthier[viii], have better relationships and be more successful[ix], along with a host of other benefits.

Happiness comes through growth and change – 'things are better than they were'. However, growth and change do not usually come from happiness. Growth and change come from an itch, a thirst, the unsettled feeling inside that tells you something isn't quite right. They come from pain and anguish, sadness and despair, and sometimes, just from a boredom that's hung around long enough to really start to bother you.

Happiness is a by-product of an uncomfortable emotion that has forced you to move. It works as part of a team to help you continue to grow and evolve in life, and to teach you to navigate hard things with a bit more peace.

Yet the hard-working coal mining cogs of the emotional ecosystem, the parts that make shit happen, don't get even half the reward or recognition big ol' Mr Happiness gets. The uncomfortable feelings get shunned and run at with pitchforks. We fight them immensely, much preferring the company of Mr H, he's such a crowd pleaser (must be a Leo).

Many of us create fear cycles as a result. We don't like letting go of things that feel good and I get it. But without the darkness we cannot have the light. And in our valiant attempts to shut out the 'bad' feelings, we end up making them worse. Fear infects our nervous systems and pops us into fight, flight, freeze, fawn or submit[x]. Which has catastrophic consequences; increasing cardiovascular risks, weakening the immune system and causing widespread inflammation throughout the body[xi].

We live in a world where we can pay for things to happen faster. Whether that's your food shop or selling your car. It's no wonder that we don't want to wait for Mr H to come back round again. It goes against what we're used to here. We can use drugs, alcohol, food, social media and more modern tools to supress, mask or attempt to generate some of the hormones involved in happiness instead, it's the best we can do!

Or so we think.

Your job is not to take away all of your pain and suffering, but to make that suffering tolerable so that you can still find a life worth living.

Meet Sad. She's a cool chic with an even cooler job. She is a messenger of emotion. Sometimes when she visits, she'll bring along her feeling pals like Loss, Disappointment and Hopelessness, especially when it's a loud message she has to put across. More often than not, Sad is the beginning of the ecosystem that generates Mr H's visit. She is the co-creator of happiness, the Founder, if you will. (Mr H is CEO). She works damn hard.

But there's a problem. People are deathly afraid of her. And rather than being thanked for her great contributions, she is shamed and locked away. It's a hard slog, and she wished people knew she was only there to help. Not to harm. It makes her work take much longer when she has to fight to be let in at all, when really, she doesn't want to be there any longer that we do.

It would be far too easy for me to say 'Just let her in! It's alright once she's in!'. But coming from a very traumatised have-to-constantly-look-after-my-nervous-system-like-a-toddler individual, I know it doesn't quite work like that. There are depths and complexities to accepting emotions Just The Way They Are that may never be fully understood by humans on this planet.

So here's where we start. We seek peace over happiness.

We ought not to seek happiness in hell, for what a ridiculous thing that is. But instead, we should attempt to seek peace with our existence here. Peace amongst the relentless torment within our souls. Peace in our weathered skin. Peace.

Seeking happiness is like chasing after your hot situationship. It's fun when it's fun, but honey, he isn't going to commit. Seeking Peace however...Peace is the comfort lover. Peace will make you chicken soup when you're down. Peace is slow and attentive and gentle. Peace will be loyal and unwavering, through thick and thin, good and bad. Peace will watch you in your worst moments and won't try and change you, won't tell you to calm down or say you're 'too sensitive'. Peace will hold you tight when the world feels impossible. Peace will sit with you and show you a safe corner when you're ready to move there. Peace will show you how to love yourself in a way you never knew you could.

And the craziest part of all? Peace is already part of you, hiding within.

Let's go seek.

LESSON 3: CRACK RIGHT OPEN

There's a famous Rumi quote that goes "The wound is the place where the light enters you".

When you're in the midst of deep suffering, the last thing many of us want to hear is that it's 'all happening for a reason', and 'you're exactly where you need to be'.

At the same time, there's many of us who thrive and function and find peace in turmoil when these quotes and sayings and proximity to meaning are thrust upon-us. *Glances at my wall, plastered with inspirational quotes and sayings, ink smudged from the tears of desperation that put them there in the first place*.

For me, this lifetime has felt a thousand years long. There has been suffering and privilege and bitterness and wonder, in so many extremes it makes me seasick. I have felt pain so deeply that often when I am misunderstood, I wish others could just know, for half a second, what it has felt like. I have a sneaky suspicion that I am not alone in that longing.

Over the last few years of seeing the world and human existence as a great big learning experiment, it has felt harder and harder to partake in it with joy. "If this is what I have to keep doing over and over again for the next 60 years, how can I possibly see it with excitement? When pain is inevitable? When the fear of 'the next hard thing' consumes me? How can I possibly look forward to that?"

Life was wearing me down. Trauma after trauma, major event after major event. I kept asking for a 'break'. I needed some time out to recover from all of it, before the next one inevitably came around. But still life came at me, like a harsh tide controlled by forces intangible. It wasn't personal. She was doing her job. I was: exactly where I was supposed to be. I just hated it at the same time. It scared me to be here.

When the body remains in a chronic state of stress or fear, our nervous system can get stuck in overdrive. We live in a permanent state of 'panic' and become so used to it that we don't even realise we're in it. This, in turn, can supress our immune system, potentially leading to a host of physical health issues such as autoimmune diseases and inflammation[xii].

As time went on, and as I could have predicted through the meticulous study of how trauma and physiology[xiii] team up (I am after all a detective of the soul, emotion and existence), my body began to break down. By my mid-twenties I had multiple diagnoses of chronic pain conditions, endocrine disorders, digestive issues and mobility restrictions, often leaving me on crutches or bedbound.

That was the final straw.

I was now staying here out of spite. The optimistic, hopeful, 'I can get through anything' soul I had come here with was now a pit of bitterness and sarcasm. I resented myself at the same time as finding it all rather endearing. "Oh no, another cancer scare" I rolled my eyes dramatically whilst furiously refreshing my blood test results page. "Oh no, another sudden death of someone close to me I wasn't expecting", I smirked through intense sobbing and smudged mascara.

My twisted perception of the world was detached and committed all at the same time. Determined but hopeless. Devoted but broken. I didn't want to die but I didn't want to live.

And it felt different to depression. It felt realistic. It felt truthful and honest. It felt like I could see things as they actually were, without poetry and pretty dresses. This was just life. Hellish and uncomfortable, with short lived moments of joy. And if you were really lucky, a sense of peace and calm as you navigated the terror of it.

I spent months investigating what had happened to the Previous Me. I opened a missing persons case and spent hours sifting through old videos, texts and journal entries hunting for clues. I preferred *her* approach; I needed *her* back. She had just as much shit to deal with but handled it with grace and humility. She was funny and free and danced with the wind and connected to her root and did everything the books told her to do because she loved life and knew she could keep handling it all.

New Me threw tantrums in car parks because she forgot to get ketchup with her Mcdonalds fries. New Me self-sabotaged, and watched herself doing it, like a sadist. New Me thrived on torturing herself with dark whirling thoughts purely to get closer to source. I wanted deeper, harder, faster. I wanted pain and suffering just to remind myself that I was still alive, that I still had autonomy and choice even though I was trapped here.

And it was New Me that was ready to write this book.

Life wears you down so it can break you right open.

It takes away all of your hopes and dreams and waves them right in front of your face at the same time, like a carrot to a donkey. It crushes your soul so hard that you have no idea who you are anymore, whilst feeling more like yourself than ever before. She will walk, stamp and steamroll all over every essence of your being if that's what it takes.

We can often feel that being broken closes our hearts, locks us away within ourselves awaiting the day someone or something will free us from our pain and torture. Only to surface, weeks, months, years later, changed and new, all by ourselves. We emerge as different versions of us with softer edges worn away at by the tide of life. Tired from the journey, but stronger too.

How many times will it take life to break you open before you realise that love will never leave?

How many times will she have to crack open your soul, back bare on a cold stone table before you see that you are always there?

You are love. You are light. Let her break you.

Being broken opens our hearts so damn wide that light doesn't have a choice – it's coming in. It's flooding you with painful truths that will make you rethink absolutely everything you ever knew about yourself. It's flooding you with harsh realities of the world we live in that all the armour you had on was sheltering you from.

That light is gushing into your soul like hot, pulsing blood through arteries, purging you of toxicity and stagnation, bringing new oxygen to every cell you own. New beginnings, new memories, new moments, new breaths.

And for a little while it is going to blind you.

The wound IS where the light enters. Eventually. When you've laid limp and lifeless long enough for it to know you're not just faking it. And it's not beautiful and glory filled and Just Like Heaven. It's ugly and messy and slow, so slow. Like a full body tattoo being etched out by a snail.

You're always going to be there, you know. And when you start to forget again, life will remind you. (It's a bad habit she's got).

Maybe it doesn't feel worth it. Maybe there is no reason. Maybe it is just not fair.

But you are always going to be there.

LESSON 4: THE ONLY WAY OUT IS THROUGH

"You are the only one who can get you out of this now" I whispered to myself in the mirror, tracing the tired lines under my eyes as the depression tick sucked all the blood out of me, again.

The People Who Don't Know will tell you it's an 'attitude problem'.

The People Who Don't Know will tell you to 'just exercise more'.

The People Who Don't Know will shove affirmations in your face, or Jesus, or powders and herbal supplements and the number of a 'great therapist they know who won't keep *pandering* to you'.

The People Who Don't Know are lucky. And I am so grateful that they don't know. I wouldn't wish that on anyone. None of us would. And, a lot of the time, they come from a place of love, and misunderstanding. And occasionally, desperation. We are human, and thankfully for most of us, we don't enjoy watching others in pain. When it's those we love, it can be intolerable.

The trouble with the greatest love of your life being inside you is that it can be really hard to get any perspective on it. On the way you beat her up without realising. Neglect how she feels. Ignore her cries for help and requests for even just a hug. We stop seeing how wonderful she is. All the things she's achieved. All the ways she lights up the world and makes it a better place here, for everyone.

We concentrate instead on pleasing the outside world. Sometimes hyper fixating on everything outside of ourselves is a well thought out distraction. Other times, it feels like the only choice. Maybe you restrict your potential as an adult because it was unsafe as a child to have strengths. To be yourself even. Maybe you don't know anything outside of saving everyone else.

Or maybe you need everyone to focus on all the good things you're doing (or even the bad things) so that no one truly sees the real you underneath.

Whatever the reason, losing connection with ourselves is not unusual. Losing sight of all the things that make us great in a world that thrives from us all *not quite being good enough* is rather understandable.

Worshipping ourselves is the unwritten forbidden law of society. And yet it might also be the cure.

There was an evil ringmaster in my brain, whip in one hand, pungent cigar in the other. He held me hostage. And because I'd neglected the relationship with myself for so long, I wasn't strong enough to defend the fort when he came charging in. There was no team. No support system. My glowing circus tent was dirty and torn, the acrobats had left, and the clown now had a drinking problem.

All day and all night the ringmaster flicked his whip at me "You need to work faster! Harder! You should be doing more! NOW! How dare you sleep! You're wasting time! Get up! Don't eat! That's for good people!".

It was exhausting. All day and all night.

And I knew that if only I could conjure up the courage to be friends, or at least acquaintances with myself, then we might have a chance at standing up to him.

But I was stubborn. And afraid. And my back was turned. And in that moment, I wouldn't even know where to start.

What does it mean to let the light in? It means surrender. And sometimes I feel like surrender is such a glorified word. 'Oh, let's just give in then, go on, it's easier'. Surrendering is often the most courageous thing a human can do. Telling ourselves to surrender involves going against the natural current of everything we've been taught to be: determined go-getters who must keep trying, always. We look up to 'heroes' who keep trying against all odds, who persevere through hardship and save the girl from the tower. We idolise the ones who sacrifice themselves to work, or service, or change. And listen, inspiration is essential for ambition (which is by no means unimportant here in the drive to love oneself.)

But what about the heroes who won by surrender? Those stories aren't exciting or dramatic enough to be told. Yet they too have courage. A lot of it.

Slogging it out and pushing through to the other side of a bad time with fire and battle doesn't always look like the hero move. Sometimes, it looks like surrendering to where we are at. Surrendering to the fact that there is absolutely nothing you can do about your situation other than sit with it and ride it out.

Sometimes letting go of chapters of us involves waving the white flag in order to move through them. Giving it all up. Losing, failing, and walking away. Pride has kept me stuck in places far too many times, when admitting defeat was often the best way forward.

You have to keep coming back to the notion that emotions need movement. Stagnation is a breeding ground for despair and inner torment. Moving through our feelings allows the uncomfortable ones to pass through and leave a trail of diamonds in their wake.

And backwards or sideways? Alternative ways out? They don't really exist. The lesson will manifest itself again and again until you get it. It makes more sense to go through with it and trust with all that you are that this experience was tailored by you, for you. That your soul knew what would crack you open, wake you up, and help you grow. That deep down in this dark moment, lessons will be learnt that will serve you forever, harsh as they may be necessary.

The journey you will undertake upon meeting the greatest love of your life will change you forever. It's not easy or smooth sailing, and it won't always make sense. The dark times may come and go, just as they did before.

But this time you will know you're not alone. You'll have you, and the boat full of love you've got waiting for you within.

And if we're heading into the impossible, we may as well do it together.

THE ONLY WAY OUT is THROUGH

LESSON 5: (YOU'RE NOT SPECIAL, IT'S NOT PERSONAL, THERE'S NO ONE COMING TO SAVE YOU).

When I was five, I vividly recall telling my mother that 'I was different' as she tucked me in to bed one night. For as long as I could remember, I didn't feel like I belonged here. My past life memories were so vivid at that age (as they often are), that I just wanted to go 'home'. The feeling of not fitting in carried through into adulthood, but by this point, I had come to terms with it, and knew that unique quirks came with 'different' that granted gifts and tools that other people didn't have.

Self-isolation however can often breed entitlement. I felt entitled to a much better pack of cards than I'd been given. I often felt like I had it harder than other people, and resented them for that, whilst allowing that gap to add to my inner isolation even more. It wasn't that I hadn't met people who had endured hardships, in fact it was almost the opposite. For whatever reason, I seemed to be able to pick out the people who 'knew pain' in a crowd. My greatest connections have been with those who've experienced messy trauma too. Yet still I believed I was different, special, that it was meant to be easier for me. I was meant for more than this.

Therapists will tell you it's a coping mechanism, my way of reaffirming hope in the dark. That it's simply my neurodivergent traits playing out. That it was because I found it hard to trust people or lacked a sense of reality from years of disassociation. I believed it was a deep soul knowing, that intuitively I knew what was coming for me, and it was better than this. Perhaps it's a combination of all of those things, perhaps it's not.

It wasn't until I began to reframe my hardcore life events as learning experiences rather than personal attacks that the intense injustice I felt began to wane. I began to recognise that my major traumas weren't because I was a 'bad human', but just part of the experience of life. And that I really could let go of my 'I guess this is just payback for all the bad things I've done' narrative. (The 'Fuck it, just do it, I'm already going to hell anyway' mindset is great fun but also quite toxic on the self-love and self-compassion frontier).

Creating that separation between 'life is out to get me' and 'life is tough and sometimes it knocks me down for a little while' is pretty critical in getting out of the victim mindset of existence. There will always be someone who has it harder, someone who has it easier, someone who is prettier, fatter, thinner, uglier etc, etc, etc. It's not personal and you're not special. You're a random player in this game, with a set of circumstances designed to give you all the learning you need whilst you're here. Along with everybody else.

If you subscribe to the past-life theory I discussed earlier in the book, where YOU choose what happens to you here based on what you know will teach you the most, then it's the opposite of a personal attack: everything is set up to guide you to your highest potential. And that is the same for everyone else hanging out here. Everyone has different lessons to learn, has different levels of soul advancement, has different core wounds to tackle. That's why none of us have the same lives. We'd never learn anything if the lessons weren't tailored to us.

If you've felt pain in this life like you never thought real or possible, then you knew yourself well enough to place that in your lifeline. You knew what would break and destroy you the most in order for you to crack right open and let the light in.

In amongst these moments (and sometimes outside of them too) we can often find ourselves just waiting to be rescued. Someone will come along and fix it all. Something will happen that will change our lives for the better. "When this happens' I'll be okay, "If that happens' it will be better, fixed, whole. And as much as I wholeheartedly and utterly believe in expecting miracles in this life, depending on them to make things better for us just will not work.

There is no one coming to get you. Except YOU.

The greatest miracle of all will be what you discover inside yourself. The strength, the light, the capacity to love in bigger ways than you even knew existed on this earth.

It's one of the toughest narratives to reframe; hope is after all our driving force. Why not let love be your driving force instead? Why not let knowing yourself be the thing that saves you? Why not find your faith through what it means to be you, and all the gifts you hold locked within?

And in this waiting for things to be better, for someone to save you, for a breath of fresh air...let it be you.

YOU are the person you always wanted to be saved by.

LESSON 6: WHAT IF YOUR PURPOSE ISN'T ACCOLADES?

I see you, sitting there, punishing yourself for all the things you haven't 'become' yet. I see you sifting through forgotten dreams and lost hopes and reminiscing over the moments where you felt a little closer to being enough.

Isn't there a part of you that loves it? Just a little bit? The constant pushing to be more? Doesn't it give you meaning sometimes? Isn't it the reason you get out of bed in the mornings?

Isn't it exhausting?

It's a heaviness that sits in the chest, the heart space. The striving and the yearning, combined with the unfaltering truth that it will never be enough for what you expect of yourself.

"You will never be enough." The voice booms inside you.

So, you work harder, faster, longer. You sacrifice rest, rest is for the weak. You speed through eating food, washing and dressing. They aren't making you productive, they're a waste. You must do more. Always more.

If you didn't completely lose yourself in the process, you'll get your accolade. You'll write the book or get that promotion or buy that house.

It might feel enough for a little while. Until it doesn't. And this time, you'll have to go bigger and better than the last. Hell, let's just give up weekends and time with family while we're here. It'll be worth it in the end... right?

Maybe your accolades look like social recognition and reputation. Maybe, if you dug deeper, all your accolades lead back to that. Maybe they're all about making your mum proud – and even when she tells you she is, it won't feel like the truth. Maybe they're about material wealth. And maybe you've achieved that, but the aching loneliness remains.

What if your destiny is just to have a beautiful life? What if the goal isn't accolades, but peace? What if the purpose all along was to simply be yourself?

How would life feel to live without all that pressure? If the only expectation you had for yourself was simply to 'be'? Can you imagine having the permission granted to actually pursue a life of fun as your purpose? Think of the things you might do, think of the things you might never do again.

Your mental health doesn't care about how rich you are. If you hate yourself then it doesn't matter how much you achieve, being a multi-millionaire is not going to be the golden ticket. I don't know that wealth, as an aspiration, is particularly healthy for our already in-pain psyche in a financial climate such as the one we live in. I am all for simple living and part-time hours if that's what makes your heart sing. I am all for having hobbies without monetising them. Lives without them needing to be on display. Careers without them being the sole description of Who You Are. You are allowed to find a different rhythm and pattern of existence than the one everyone else follows. That's okay.

Who we are 'on paper', e.g. Graham the biggest earning lawyer in the county, will mean nothing when we are no longer that thing. When Graham retires, Graham will be known to all who pass by as Graham the old man. When Mikela's eyesight deterioration means she can no longer drive the neon pink pimped up range-rover, she will just be Mikela, who can't drive.

Who we are inside however, will remain. Graham the warm-hearted old man. Mikela who speaks kindly to herself. Graham who has taught himself to not just be comfortable living alone since his wife died, but to enjoy and thrive in his own company. Mikela who continues to pursue her creative passions in different and unique ways after her eyesight changed, because she is adaptable, and sees things as challenges to learn from, not punishments against her by a 'greater power'.

You will never be enough for you as long as you base your happiness on how productive you are. If we can let go of the people we think we should be, and find contentment instead with the people we are (all the messy, incomplete and learning to blossom parts and all), then joy can be allowed in. Peace can be allowed in.

The true self, can be allowed in.

LESSON 7: YOU ARE ALREADY CHANGING THE WORLD.

At the very start of my career existentialism, I was passed around some family friends on a wisdom gathering exercise, in the hope that perhaps something might 'click'. All these individuals were successful in their own right, (at least to a teenager working at £6 an hour in retail anyway) with a vast scope of life experience and knowledge across the board. I didn't know what I wanted to be, or do, and this experiment was to see if we could find any answers, for everyone's sakes. It's stressful in this world when you have no set career path. It's a feeling we feel we should already have. We feel we should have been born with it, like your friend Callum who always wanted to work with food and is now a famous Patisserie chef in Paris. Why can't we be like him?

All of them asked me the same things; "What do you want to do with your life?", "What do you enjoy doing?", and "What are you good at?".

My replies looked like this; I wanted to change the world. I loved writing, cooking, and being with animals. And I was pretty good at those things too.

"You can't change the world" one said, "so take that ambition out of your mind right away."

"It's unlikely you'll make a career of writing" said another "it's best you just leave that as a hobby."

"There's no money in working with animals, is there anything else you have skills in?"

As the boring, dull adult I too have become, they weren't entirely wrong. I, having nothing else to bet on, took their advice. Writing has remained my hobby, my passion, my secret love affair (now shared with an online community of like-minded creative beans), and although it would be nice, I have no expectations of the thing I love the most to provide the roof over my head.

I tried my hand in the culinary world, and even became a cake decorator for a short while. But alas, the joy I once felt for cooking waned, when something you love becomes something you have to do, the passion often withers and dies. Adulthood frightened the fun foods out of me too, one minute bacon was going to kill you, the next avocados. It just wasn't the same anymore.

And working with animals? One of the most heart-wrenching, soul-crushing, underpaid and overworked jobs I have ever done. The cute and fluffy side wears off as quickly as the novelty of puppies in lockdown did. It wasn't for the faint hearted.

But there's one thing that did work out, rather unexpectedly in fact. Changing the world. And discovering my greatest talent: sharing my truths and being vulnerable.

With the introduction of social media, everyday folks like myself have had the opportunities to reach big audiences across the world. The words I have shared from my soul have been read by thousands and watched by many more. But this isn't what I'm talking about.

All of us are out here changing the world, right now. Perhaps we aren't making huge global shifts in narrative overnight, but we are radically transforming our own small corners of this place. We are teaching each other a new way of being. Of learning. Of growing.

We are starting conversations now that haven't been had for hundreds, maybe thousands of years. We are talking about the essence of what it is to be human, outside of faith, outside of our careers, outside of what the weather is like today. We are talking about self-development outside of ambition, and talking personal growth for the collective uplifting of others. We are talking about raising our children in a trauma-informed, mindful way.

We are talking about how our BODY feels. We are talking about how our MIND feels. We are sharing now a deeper compassion for mental health than ever before in recorded history. We are understanding trauma, breaking generational cycles and setting boundaries (insert sassy finger *click click* here). Some of us are even talking about having better SEX. Who would've known!

We are slowly but surely bringing back our intuition. The powerful, almost magical creatures we are deep down underneath the 'fluff' of distraction from the self are starting to reveal themselves, and radical evolution into better humanity will begin to follow.

We are learning to trust ourselves based not on whether we fit into societies modelling, but on whether our gut says we are heading in the right direction. The shift in narrative is happening. And you are playing a part in that.

By encouraging conversations like this in your own circles, you are changing the world. Little old you IS changing the entire narrative of the way this planet and the people on it are evolving.

In sharing your inner truths and getting vulnerable, you encourage others to do the same. And help us realise en masse that there is so much more to all of this than just existing. We are love. We are light. We are great forces of hope and change and transformation.

Even if these kinds of conversations are new and uncomfortable to you, look at you getting curious. Look at you exploring it all. Look at you thinking about it. I hope you are proud.

So I don't want you to sit here and feel like you're not enough anymore. You're a world changer hunny. We all are. And we are all so very necessary for levelling up humanity, and all the potential we have yet to discover.

YOU ARE

AMAZING

IN EVERY

WAY

PART 2: OTHERS

In the early days of 2020, after a fateful Boxing Day that almost ended my life, I left a long and drawn-out abusive relationship. In the space of three and half years, I had become someone I no longer recognised. My face was tired and pale, my body bruised and fragile. I had given up my autonomy, thrown it away by this point in fact, because it was too hard to keep holding onto something so visceral when my only focus had become everyday physical survival.

I didn't know it then, but the process of self-discovery and reclamation that followed was going to change my life.

For the duration of that relationship, I had given myself to friends and family in a way I never had before. It was my greatest distraction at the time. I had built connections that reaffirmed my ability to socialise for the sake of community, which was a big change from how I'd perceived social connection in my teen years.

In my teens, isolated and lonely, I'd taken to sex and alcohol to find connection when I didn't know how. Men were my target. I was manipulative and controlling, using sex as my superpower, giving me the illusion of control after all the years I'd felt I had none. I wanted to reclaim what had been taken from me in my early years as a childhood sexual abuse survivor – my body, my control, my consent. But unfortunately, I ended up losing it entirely, all over again. And on a Thursday, another man took my lifeless, bleeding body, and claimed it as his own as I once again, screamed out: "STOP!".

In the shadows of that era, my fragile and vulnerable low self-esteem created different relationships with men: non-sexual friendships. This was new and strange to me, and the novelty took me straight into a relationship that I didn't give myself time to question. Somebody cared for me outside of what my body was worth. Somebody gave me their time and attention (albeit on his terms, but who was I to question that, I was lucky enough to get anything). And with that came those new friendships, my lifeline. I connected with his family and friends and played the role of gift bearer and companion. I was liked and popular, they had time for my stories and the energy I had that had always been ignored and seen as 'too much' in previous social circles. I cared for them, and I liked it.

My own family at that time held conflict and unhealed wounds. There was silence and anger, confusion and resent. I couldn't hold space without rage. I couldn't listen without questioning what was real and what was not. I had a lot of my own work to do. I had to learn boundaries, energetically, emotionally and physically. I wasn't ready to integrate back with them yet.

My new social group, who, unaware of the way my secretly toxic relationship was slowly destroying me, took me on board and showed me what connection meant.

In the early days of 2020 however, all of that came crashing down.

Loyalties are not always just, or fair, or right. Sometimes they come with threats and callous words and accusations. Sometimes the innocent are branded in blood simply because they risk unsettling the system. Bringing truths to light that will change everything. Shaking up reputations and tearing down false foundations; folly castles.

The perfect man they knew and loved could not possibly be a violent abuser with a strangulation fetish. I was the problem. The holes in the wall and the furniture must have been my tiny fists. The bruises and hospital stays must have been my own doing.

Overnight my bubbling social life was shattered as I courageously decided to choose freedom, and as the pain of betrayal seeped through my blood, I questioned how I could ever trust people again.

*

It's three years later and I'm buying my sister breakfast in a café by the sea. A man who treasures me and the dog of my dreams are sat by my side too, gassing away in different forms, (you can figure out which was which). I'm so absorbed in the conversation that I've forgotten anybody else is in here. The laughter is so wholesome it doesn't matter anyway. It's all worth it.

I'm depressed and feel like I have been for years, is it any surprise? But this moment let me forget it all. Everything feels light here. The sips of Chai Latte explode in my mouth as we reminisce old holidays in the sun, and my boyfriend points out how we both had to burst our egg yolks as soon as our breakfasts arrived. "Huh, she does that too." He said, perplexed and touched by our subtle similarities.

I'd withdrawn from others for the last few years, with the exception of the iconic healthy romantic relationship my newfound patience and slow healing had allowed me to cultivate, we'll get to that later. I'd spent Christmas's in complete solidarity in cabins on Scottish mountaintops. Ended old friendships and taken long breaks from communicating with my family. Lived for months by the ocean without seeing another human for weeks at a time.

All to get back to here – objectivity.

I had to see relationships and interactions without the bias of my sentient mind. Without assumptions and interference from what I thought they meant. It had to be stripped right back. It had to be about us, not me, not them, but us. I had to ask myself 'Is this relationship energetically beneficial to me? And to them?' and if not, 'Is this relationship or interaction here to teach me something?'

'Is it a lesson, or a blessing?'

Prior to this, social interactions had meant neither of those things. They looked more like people pleasing, attention seeking and approval hunting. Or worse, they were fear driven. I hadn't realised any of this until I'd truly stepped outside of it all and perceived myself through the eyes of an observer.

Without realising it, the cynicism I'd developed towards life had helped heal my relationships with others. Creating the distance between us had united us. And allowed entire new friendships and foundations to be built within the ruins of the old ones.

I may no longer have a long list of Christmas cards to write, and I may not get to go to regular social gatherings and flirt with group energy anymore. But I do know authenticity now. I know who is worth my time, and how I can help them too. I choose friendships and connections because I want to bring value, rather than because I need something from them or feel like I have to be there.

Can it be that spending time living in the darkness inside your mind brings the most clarity of all? And can it be that social connection, when done authentically in every aspect, can offer magical moments of healing and great learning opportunities, for both parties?

I think so. I think others can be our mirrors should we be willing to learn. Others, consciously or subconsciously, through love or hate, can teach us things about ourselves that will evolve us into greater versions of who we are.

There is mighty power in connection. There might even be a necessity for it, with multiple studies now showing good quality social connections to have a significant impact on life expectancy[xiv].

The behaviour of others can often be what breaks us. They can also be a catalyst for great self-evolution and change. They can show us the best and worst parts of ourselves. They can remind us that boundaries are necessary and loving. And equally, that intimacy is too.

The others are here as guides and often teachers. We just have to look at them from the right angle.

LESSON 8: IF YOU'RE NOT FULL OF YOURSELF, WHAT ARE YOU FULL OF?

I am the most selfish person I know. And I carry so much darn guilt about it that it eats me alive and mutates into depressive episodes. But pain and isolation have been my teachers. Loneliness was my only friend for a long time. And when you do it solo for so long, you see things differently. You tune in more to your own consciousness. You realise that a lot of the activities you would have called 'selfless' before, were actually just for self-gratification, virtue signalling, because 'everyone else was doing it so I felt like I had to'. Or because it would take away the guilt of some of the bad things you've done.

People love to throw the word 'selfish' around. It's powerful to call people selfish. You suddenly become more righteous, better, proper. Across history, stories of helping others are paraded through the crowds. More heroes whose intentions we will never truly know.

You see, if my familiarity of selfishness has taught me anything, it's this:

The truest acts of selflessness, of genuine care with no want or desire for anything in return, no fear of the consequences if you didn't do it, the truest acts come from those who have filled themselves up with so much self-love that it is overflowing, and they have some to spare.

Let's bring some old friends in: 'Put your oxygen mask on first', 'You can't pour from an empty cup', 'Being selfish is selfless'.

Just because helping other people is a kind thing, doesn't always mean that it is backed by kind intentions. Time is precious and fleeting, and often there is no benefit to giving it away. Often we can feel resentful about giving, especially if it hasn't come from an authentic place. Which is fine, that's life.

But imagine if it could come from an authentic place? Imagine a joy (and peace) roaring so loudly within you that all you wanted to do was share it, so everyone else could feel it too.

It is absolutely possible.

And that is my sales pitch on why we should be selfish and love ourselves relentlessly until we're so full of love we BURST.

Unfortunately, being selfish means that everyone will hate you. Okay, not everyone, *some* people will fixate on how wrong you are in their eyes. Doing what we've always known reminds us of comfort and safety, even if it is wrong or outdated. Herd mentality and conformist behaviour comes through a combination of fear and comfort. If someone tries to disrupt that – even if it doesn't directly affect us- it can be extremely unnerving, even threatening.

And we are social, people pleasing beans that struggle with being disliked massively. Breaking societal norms is a huge deal, and there's no guidebook to the rollercoaster of emotions it can bring. From liberation and empowerment to shame and self-doubt all in the same moment.

There is also a fine-tuned art to selfishness in the name of self-love. You do have to be at least a little bit conscious about not being a total jerk to everyone around you, whilst being a little bit bold about setting boundaries with others at the same time. I would argue though that any art can be mastered with practice and willingness to learn.

And please, tell me, where would we be today if throughout history people hadn't broken societal norms, and within that set the ball rolling for some of the biggest cultural movements in history? If no one had made that first move, wouldn't hundreds of thousands of people still be socially or physically enslaved by societies faulty traditions and rituals?

So even if you have no self-love role models right now, YOU can make the first move. You can be daring and courageous and afraid – that's all part of the process. Allow yourself to change your perspective of selfishness and see it as honourable instead of self-indulgent. (Although honestly, I'm all here for self-indulgence).

One of the biggest cons that society has forced upon us is that keeping us small and resentful to ourselves is helpful for other people. Instead, it's a method of control, it keeps us quiet and well-behaved and unquestioning.

If you're not full of yourself, what are you full of? Shame? Greed? Envy? FEAR?

In reality, being selfish shows you exactly what you have the potential to bring to this world. Yes, that's right, to everybody else. The gift you have to share will be shown to you when you fill your cup so full you can't keep it in anymore. And then everybody wins. We all get a handout. You will become a fountain of riches. People will see how real and pure and true it is, and that it is a possibility for them too.

Until you *choose you*, there is no great shift. And you will carry the guilt, and sometimes it will eat you alive like it does for me. But that won't last forever. It is a process. A marathon, not a sprint.

All you have to do is start.

You Won't
Find A Home
Outside of yourself
Until You Find One
Within

LESSON 9: BUT CULTURE MAKES IT SO

It was a weathered 52-year-old Shakespeare who originally wrote the famous quote, "There is nothing either good or bad but thinking makes it so" in his bitter tragedy Hamlet. Of course, there is lots to unpack here. I'm from the school of thinking that just telling people to 'think better thoughts' is too simplistic and doesn't consider individual circumstances. Although I have no doubt that a powerful self-discipline and motivation routine a day keeps the doctor away, it's also not an option for everyone.

But if we looked at this quote from a broader point of view, involving morals and what is 'socially acceptable', who are we to think we can determine what is good or bad in this world?

Having standards of 'good behaviour' gives people power and safety, safety and power. How we 'should' behave, what is considered 'righteous' and 'pure', are merely society's way of keeping us under control.

Good people can do evil things and evil people can do good things. Tarnishing someone as good or bad based on whether they fit into the culturally acceptable ways of the world seems kind of backwards, don't you think?

A school shooter for example can destroy lives in a matter of minutes. The implications of one person's behaviour can detrimentally affect hundreds of people's lives and send shockwaves through a community. I know this is a painful question, but does this mean they are an evil person? Do we really know enough to answer that? What if this person had been abused for years and years, neglected by peers and family for being aloof and reclusive, when actually they were just hurting immensely inside?

And what about the person that abused them? They must be evil, right? They are who we should direct our anger to, surely? But I ask again, do we really know enough to answer that? What's their story? Perhaps they were sex trafficked for the first 20 years of their life? Or grew up in extreme poverty with alcoholic parents. We just don't know. And even if we do, is it enough? Can we truly determine if a person is good or bad based on the life events they have experienced, behaviours they have created or actions they have undertaken?

And likewise, can we really say that the public figure, or even local hero who spends all their time raising money for charity and bringing awareness to desperate causes doesn't molest children on the side, or practice tax evasion, or bullied someone into taking their life? Even if they had done none of those things, how can we possibly determine someone else's intentions, thoughts and feelings behind their behaviours if we are not physically inside their head? And even if we WERE inside their head (my gosh, that would be uncomfortable), would we, mere mortal as we are, truly be able to say 'this is a saintly being'? Do we truly think ourselves powerful and knowledgeable enough to be the judge of life?

Who are we to think we can determine who, or what is good or bad in this world?

Social culture goes through waves of righteousness, which is heavily influenced by social media, of course. Acts of virtue signalling are littered across the place, from people who often don't even understand what they're virtue signalling about. They do know however, that social credit is important to keep them relevant, and protected from being 'cancelled'.

How many of these statements, I wonder, come from fear rather than strength? How many of these statements are merely duplicates, copying and pasting views and opinions because social culture says it's so? You have the power to liberate yourself from this dictatorship and protect your peace. You don't have to engage at all. Really, you don't.

Not being a conformist doesn't make you a bad person, a rebel or a hippie, it just makes you a person who makes their own choice.

And that will look different in every family, every town, every country, every workplace, every relationship. Social culture changes so quickly it's hard to keep up with it. So, don't. The more authentic you can be with yourself, the more truthful you can be with your life and the more comfortable it will become to be a human.

I want you to think for a minute about a public figure you really dislike. Then, I want you to ask yourself 'why'? If it is based on something they have done, where did you hear that information? Could you reliably fact check it? Provide valid sources?

Then I want you to ask yourself if you dislike them on behalf of YOU, or of someone else? Do you think this person behaves like this all the time? Do you think they are rotten to their core? Or could there be more going on that what it looks like? Could the media have a big influence on your opinion of this person?

Even deeper still, what is the core wound their behaviour/attitude/general presence has triggered in you? What is being mirrored here? What do they have that you lack, and vice versa? What part of your body feels activated when you think about them? Have you looked at the other side? The articles 'for' AND 'against'? Could you see this from a different perspective? Could you see how they could be interpreted differently and why?

And then, repeat this exercise for a public figure you really admire.

Perhaps everything is not as it seems. Perhaps nobody is truly good or bad. Perhaps our thoughts, and the outer influences that can affect them, are our malfunctioning markers of morals. Perhaps there are ways we can be more truthful to what feels good and right to us.

Perhaps this looks like questions, so many questions. Perhaps this looks like open-mindedness, curiosity and self-exploration. Perhaps this looks like taking people off the pedestal, but also off the floor.

It's your choice how you view your world and everything that's in it, and whether you approach challenging emotions with curiosity or criticism. *Most* of the time anyway (depression and anxiety have slightly different agendas, and freedom of thought often doesn't work in the same way, as is the case with many other mental health conditions).

We must seek compassion for ourselves wherever we are in the process of liberation from moral righteousness, in a world that decides its direction based on pop culture and the latest –sponsored by big Corp - celebrity fads.

Take time to get to know your own moral truths, and you never know, you might surprise yourself.

LESSON 10: IT'S NOT ME, IT'S YOU. IT'S NOT YOU, IT'S ME.

As the Queen of self-sabotage, I used to take everybody else's actions personally, assuming in an instant that if somebody was in an 'off mood' (my fellow empaths get it), I had done something seriously wrong. I would become fixated on all the ways I might have made a mistake and would rather make myself sick with worry than actually ask them what was up.

The self-absorption was self-harm in disguise. The more faults I found with who I was, the more I could punish myself for existing as the worthless human I believed myself to be.

I was so intensely involved in my own torture methods I hadn't even stopped to think that it might have nothing to do with me at all.

Do you remember the first time you saw one of your schoolteachers at the supermarket or the cinema, and were completely in shock that they had normal, human lives just like you? With other characters in their lives and places they existed outside of school and complexities you couldn't even vision?

Or the first time you realised as child that a grown up around you was having a tough time?

Well, it's kind of like that, except that most of the time, what goes on behind the scenes in people's lives is not public knowledge. (With exceptions such as myself, who shares everything with you, from the name of my ASDA delivery driver to the intimate details of my miscarriage).

For all you know, the man that just aggressively beeped you for leaving a junction too slowly could've just lost both his kids in a plane crash. Or the woman who is constantly patronising you at work could be battling through a complex infertility journey. The guy who keeps breaking into people's cars at night could be a challenged ex-veteran with PTSD. It's not me, it's you. And that's okay sometimes. It happens.

People often grieve for years. Just because something traumatic might not be happening right now in their lives doesn't mean it's not still causing them pain. It's never an excuse for bad behaviour, we all know that. But we don't live in a perfect world. People mess up. People get lost. People lose themselves. And people project their shit.

We cling onto our pain because we're scared of losing it. Pain reminds us that once we had love, joy, hope, naivety. And now we only have our bitter, grieving selves, it's all that's left. Without it, there is nothing.

Sometimes we hold onto our pain because we feel that if we let it go too quickly it isn't valid. We need people to see how hard it has been, how much we have been through, and how vulnerable we feel as a result. It gives an open explanation to all of the cracks in who we are as people.

I used to introduce myself with my pain first, in the hope that people would understand why I had all the flaws I did. I figured there would be no questions or criticisms if I used my pain as an excuse for my insecurities. I figured people would just 'leave me alone' and not want to dive in more if I put it all out on the table straight away. (Apologies to all the cashiers who ever asked me 'How are you today?' during a midweek meltdown food shop in my crisis years).

Sometimes there is so much pain that it does bubble over, and as social humans we have to find a way to navigate this when it does happen, without taking it as a direct assault on our own character.

The first step is detaching enough from a relationship, be that with friends, colleagues or family, to focus only on what has actually been communicated. Making the assumption that someone is annoyed at you based off non-verbal communication, (such as sulking) and then spending the rest of the day/week worrying about it is a massive drain on your energy.

Perhaps they *are* sulking about something you have done? But without that information being communicated to you, how can you determine what the issue was, if it really is about you, and how much of the issue they have is as a result of their own insecurities and projections? Why waste worry on the unknown?

Self-awareness is a blessing, but self-awareness based on your own biased assumptions is like assuming someone's food order before they've decided on it. Sometimes you'll get it right and sometimes you'll get it really, really wrong.

It is simply best to just ask. To communicate.

And this is the same when the roles are reversed. You cannot expect somebody to know how they have upset you without communicating it to them. Even if it feels obvious. Because even the most obvious hurt may mean something different to you emotionally. Are you *really* upset that they ignored your text, or is it because it's triggered a childhood abandonment wound for you? Is it *really* about the text they've ignored, or is it that *you* haven't set clear enough boundaries in the relationship itself about what's acceptable for you? Isn't it just about communication? Isn't that on you?

See what I mean?

The resentment we feel for other people can often simply be our OWN reactions to someone else's actions – not their actions themselves. It's not you, it's me. And that's okay too, we're learning. Resentment comes from love without boundaries.

For a long time, I harboured anger and resent over the actions of people in my past. So many years clinging onto anger in the hope that it would make things right. So much time wasted holding myself back by letting resent devour my identity. I believed that if no one was angry about it then it might get forgotten, the injustice brushed under the carpet, the perpetrator getting off the hook.

But I realised that the only person I was giving grief to in holding onto all of this was myself. And when I looked even deeper, I realised that a large part of the anger that I felt was actually about the actions I took as a result of theirs. It was on me. And it was one of the hardest things I've ever had to admit to myself.

This is my resent – to myself. Their actions were merely a catalyst for it, not the cause or who should be held accountable. Blame is easy. Blame gives us control and removes us from the equation. When in reality, even in the most painful and complicated of situations, we have often had some role to play in our own suffering.

I think it's brave to admit that. And from this you may grow.

LESSON 11: WE WERE ALL CHILDREN ONCE

Sometimes people can do really nasty, unforgiveable things. Forgiveness can feel impossible, and the hatred you feel for them and the way they have affected your life can consume everything you do.

Something that has helped me calm the waves of anger in situations like this is to remind myself that once upon a time they were a child too. They too were looking for approval in the eyes of their parents, learning how to play with peers, or perhaps alone. They too found excitement in new textures, colours, smells and sounds. They too found joy in the small things, like butterflies or muddy puddles.

They too learned to read and write, what the tiny glistening dots in the night sky are and that it's best to stay out of thunderstorms in case the lightening comes.

And then something went wrong. Innocence was replaced with bitterness. Curiosity with fear. Compassion with resent. And we all know how the rest goes.

Some children are put through things no human being should ever have to go through, and then expected to live life as well-behaved moral citizens without any knowledge on how to navigate the pain they feel. Without any training on how to shut the horrible flashbacks out, or trust people, or love.

Yet, as soon as they become adults, the sympathy and compassion we feel for children who have been through horrible things turns to impatience and judgement. Even for children who haven't experienced 'major' childhood trauma, but were not loved in a safe way, life can be hard as an adult.

Alcoholics, for example, are seen as reckless, out of control and lacking discipline, rather than children who were never shown how to live life alongside pain, so used alcohol to numb it. One study found that 62% of adults in an alcoholism treatment study had experienced physical or sexual abuse as a child[xv]. This doesn't include trauma these individuals may have experienced in adulthood either.

And although this process of thinking can't right the wrongs, it can allow us to reframe the way somebody else's actions are consuming us.

When you look at the cruelty that has been done to you by another, can you imagine how much they must be hurting to do something like that? How bitter and cold their life must be to want to inflict that same pain onto you? How much pain must have been stagnating and building inside themselves to mutate into the actions it did? Can you, somewhere deep within, find sympathy for the life that has been taken away from them? The chances of joy stripped bare and replaced with pain. Can you feel sorry for them that this is the only way the feel they can behave to remain safe here on this planet?

Can you recognise that the deep mistrust they have for others has only come from a deep betrayal or lack of trust from situations in their own lives?

Can you walk with courage and bravery and pride at the knowledge that you chose to take your pain on yourself without inflicting it on another? That you want to move through it and that you have the strength deep-down inside to do that?

Can you walk with courage and bravery and pride and forgive yourself for any pain you have inflicted on someone else? Can you, with time and healing and reconciliation, relieve yourself from that guilt – with the knowledge that you too were a child once, just trying to get it all right. Just trying to keep yourself safe. Just trying to survive.

Sympathy is a much less consuming emotion than anger. Sympathy comes from a place of love and compassion. And in this case, a place of healing, and choosing to do so.

Bad behaviour can never be excused, but it can often be understood. You owe yourself the chance to try and understand. You owe yourself the chance to try and shift that anger. Feel it, then diffuse it. Stomp it out through your feet and scream it to the open hills.

Because you were also a child once. And injustice hurts in the same way it hurt you then too. We are just humans, trying to figure out how to navigate big feelings.

And how to allow ourselves to do so.

OUR WORST HABITS WERE ONCE OUR BEST ATTEMPTS TO MAKE OURSELVES FEEL SAFE

LESSON 12: I'M NOT INTIMIDATING, YOU'RE INTIMIDATED

As a recovering people pleaser, I'm still growing into this one. I'm still trying to feel safe in saying 'no' and 'I don't want to' and 'I'm not comfortable with that'. I'm still conjuring up the courage to not engage with people just because the terrified voice in my head says I should.

Setting boundaries does not make you a bad person. I'll say that again. Setting boundaries does not make you a bad person. Nor does being assertive. Nor does speaking your truth.

As a veteran moral perfectionist, when people set boundaries with me in the past it sent me right into defence. My body would panic "I've done something wrong! And we all know what happens when I do something wrong, I get punished!" (please insert your own 'what happened when you did something wrong as a child' wiring here). Often, I would fawn and be 'too nice', scared of the consequences of 'breaking the rules'. Sometimes I would even get critical.

But that was my issue. I was intimidated.

That was nothing to do with the person who had set the boundaries with me.

The people who set the boundaries are respecting their energy. Respecting their rights. Respecting themselves. And what an honourable thing that is.

And it could be you, my fellow people pleaser.

I encourage you to stop explaining why you can't work that overtime shift next week. Just say 'sorry, no'.

I encourage you to stop explaining why you can't attend the family party you know will drain your energy. Just say 'no thank you'.

I encourage you to start listening to yourself better 'I'm not feeling up to a walk today, how about a duvet day?'

I encourage you to stop explaining why.

You don't owe anyone an explanation for the boundaries that are relevant and specific to you. It's like people asking for your medical history – it's none of their business.

The first time you do it, it's going to feel hella uncomfortable. You might overthink and consider unsending the text and just generally freak out (been there, done that). But then, it'll get easier…and you'll be able to apply it to even more areas of your life.

Don't like small talk? Fuck it off. Redirect the conversation, e.g. "Yes, bleak out there, but anyway, how are you, really?"

Don't want to be replying to work emails on weekends? Put it in your email signature. Here's what mine looks like:

"Please Note: I will not engage in work emails after 7 pm or on weekends and aim to get back to you within 3 working days. I don't expect you to read, reply, or take any action about this outside of your normal working hours."

Don't have the energy for a certain conversation with a certain person right now? Let them know. e.g. "I'm not in the right frame of mind to talk about this right now, can we discuss this another time?"

Dealing with relatives who often say hurtful things to you? Don't ignore it, approach it, e.g. "That's an odd thing to say, did you mean to say that out loud?" or "Hmm, I didn't like what you just said, can you explain what you meant by that? I wouldn't want to misinterpret it."

Or my absolute favourite one-liner that can be used for almost any boundary setting situation: "I'm at capacity right now".

And people won't like it. Just like I didn't the first times people set boundaries with me. People will respond in a huge variety of different ways if their nervous system gets activated (specifically fight, flight, freeze, fawn, attach[xvi]). It will be frightening to feel like you have upset someone. So, you have to keep reminding yourself that their response is not about you, but them. You aren't being intimidating, you are just being clear on your boundaries. It is their responsibility to handle what you have said. It is their responsibility to manage their reaction. Not yours.

Setting boundaries is a huge step forward in living as your authentic, uninterrupted, perfectly imperfect self.

LESSON 13: NO ONE OWES YOU AIRTIME

My wiring for communication and conversation (as someone who massively struggles to trust people) has meant I have often perceived social interactions as transactional. An eye for an eye. An 'I'll listen to your fifteen-minute rant about your love life if you listen to mine'. An 'If he's listening to me, he must want something from me' approach. It's taken a lot of learning and unlearning to recognise that transactional conversations are not stable foundations for building social relationships and are generally limited to sales personnel and narcissists.

I would often find myself sat listening 'in the wings' in conversations, waiting for my turn to perform and be heard, then walking away frustrated when I was never given that opportunity. There was no part of me that could accept the conversation wasn't about me – making it about them would mean that I cared about them, which wasn't going to happen, because caring meant trusting, and trusting meant letting people in.

Eventually I hit a point in my healing journey where I began to recognise myself drifting off during these conversations. Noticing this encouraged me to question my behaviour, dive deep into the whys and what's, and try and understand how I could navigate these situations safely, both for my nervous system and for the individuals in my life.

Honestly, the most important step was removing myself from conversations and interactions with people that didn't make me feel safe. I wasn't healed enough to tackle that bridge at that time, and the most sensible thing to do was to take some time out. This isn't a matter of just walking away from conversations that don't interest you, it's deeper than that. This part is about tuning into your own energy and recognising how communicating with someone makes you feel inside.

Are your shoulders tense when you are talking to them? Is your chest tight, or are your fists clenched without you realising? Do you notice the tone of your voice change around them, or even the volume? Do you come away from this person feeling calm or on edge? Do you dread communicating with them, or perceive it as a chore or burden?

If any of these issues flag up, it's worth taking some space. It may be nothing to do with them, it may be your own nervous system struggling to regulate, but continuing to put yourself in what your body considers to be an unsafe environment will not heal that wound without some inner work first.

Then I was left with the people I did feel safer with (you will never feel safe around *anyone* until you feel safe within your body). With these individuals, I began to allow myself to listen compassionately for the sake of listening compassionately. I began to recognise how much they needed it, how much it was helping them and how just listening alone didn't mean they were penetrating my soul and all my vulnerabilities, it was just a nice thing to do.

I became a lot more present in conversations, asking questions and genuinely wanting to know more about their problems, and find out what the individual needed in those moments to ease the pain. I used empathy developed from my own traumas to connect with people on a different level. I helped them feel seen in all the ways I wished I had been, and it felt so good to be able to give that time and energy.

I saw what had happened – I had gone from needing to dominate conversations to avoid anyone trying to dive into my soul, to giving all of my soul and being vulnerable in order to help others heal. It was a complete 360. I no longer wanted the airtime; I got such a kick from helping other people now instead. (Still found a way to make it about me, eh? But this is quite a human thing.)

No one owes you airtime. You don't give a gift to someone just because you want a gift back. You do it because you care, and making them happy makes you happy. Often far happier than receiving a gift (or airtime) yourself.

This is still a work in progress for me. How to communicate authentically in person, whilst maintaining boundaries and recognising when someone is no good for you. Trusting people in general may always be a work in progress for trauma survivors. And that's okay. The point is progress, which won't always be linear or straightforward.

It's still progress.

LESSON 14: HOW IT MADE YOU FEEL DOESN'T MEAN IT IS THE TRUTH

There's a confidence that comes with strong emotions that often prevents us from seeing things objectively – from the outside. Emotion can be so convincing that there need be no other evidence to prove its validity. No other form of questioning, no more sweeping for clues. The Jury decides before the case is even tried. That is how strong feelings can be.

But there's another side to this story, and that's truth. And this is a harsh pill to swallow – I'm cool if you feel a little defensive about this one, I sure did.

Sometimes (and we've talked about this briefly already) the way you feel after interpersonal conflict may not be down to the event itself, but the trigger it has activated, and the feelings that sit behind, waiting and ready to jump out at you when they're called. Sometimes we can get really lost in the pain and harbour anger and resent at someone when actually, if you really asked yourself what was going on, the feelings are coming from within you – not from what they did. It is *your* reaction to their action.

I believe in validating feelings. You feel angry? Yes, you do. You can own that while it's there, that's cool. That is YOUR TRUTH. There is absolutely no denying that. Feelings are real and raw and important.

They are messengers, processing tools. Feelings are a key part of the inner processing of life.

Let's play with a slightly elaborate example here, which may or may not be based on my own true story, and the conversation I had with myself as a result:

Why do you feel angry?

Because they went home early on a night out, saying they didn't feel well, leaving me on my own. We'd been planning this for weeks. They seemed fine!

That's frustrating, I can understand why you'd be angry. Now let's go deeper. Why did that make you angry?

Because the plan was that we would stay together the whole night, I really needed this break right now to get away from everything going on in my life. I stayed out of spite, to prove I didn't need them to have fun, but I ended up tripping over and spraining my ankle. It wouldn't have happened if they were there, they always look out for me.

Now let's go back over that answer and find out how much of that anger is actually about the friend that went home early... *'I* really needed this.' *'I* stayed out of spite, to prove *I* didn't need them'. *'I* tripped over'.

You were abandoned. That can trigger a lot. You had been looking forward to a release of some of the tension you'd been experiencing recently and feel let down that you weren't able to do that. You feel that you wouldn't have injured yourself (through reckless intoxicated abandon...supposedly) if your friend had been there looking out for you. But the part that's missing is the truth – it wasn't personal. They hadn't planned to feel unwell. You have no idea what else could be going on right now with them.

You 'needed to get away from everything'. That isn't your friend's problem. They can support you as best they can, but it is not their responsibility to get you out of dark places. It's yours. They shouldn't sacrifice their wellbeing for you, they need to put their mask on first before helping others, as do you.

You 'stayed to prove you could do it on your own'. You used hyper-independence as a coping mechanism in response to feeling abandoned. Is this a behaviour pattern you may have used before, or even in childhood? Our worst habits were once our best attempts to make ourselves feel safe, this moment, being retriggered, is no exception. You were trying to make yourself feel safe again, and it was the best outcome you could think of at the time. Your body had good intentions.

Although every scenario involving strong emotions and interpersonal conflict like this will be different and have its own set of unique and complex circumstances, hopefully this example can open your eyes a little to the way feelings can present themselves to us – and how they aren't always to be trusted as point-blank evidence to a scenario. E.g. I am angry at them therefore they are a terrible person.

Of course, there are times when someone else's behaviour *is* directly correlating with the emotion you feel, that sucks, I'm sorry. The boundaries chapter is useful here. And maybe some deep healing, which we are about to dive into.

On a much lighter note – think of how differently you perceive emotions when you are tired, cold or hungry? Everything is exacerbated. Everything seems more serious. Your body's priority is survival, not happiness or truth seeking – that's up to our minds to intervene.

So the next time you're about to let yourself spiral into an angry whirlwind because of someone else's behaviour, or a pit of guilt, pool of sorrow, ask yourself this:

"What is this really about?"

PART 3: LOSS & CRISIS

There is something reassuring about hitting rock bottom.

When I was seventeen my best friend died. I cried on the carpet to Coldplay. I didn't eat. Didn't sleep. Didn't go to school or know how to function. All I knew how to do in those moments was cry on the floor to Coldplay.

A year later, to the week, in fact, I was brutally raped by a stranger and left to bleed out. The sexual abuse I had experienced as a child was retriggered, and I cried in the bath to Coldplay with a bottle of rum every night for weeks and weeks and weeks. Hoping one day my body would be clean enough to forget it all.

At 20, the sudden tragic death of my young dog, the only hope I felt I had in amidst a violent abusive relationship, drove me to attempt to take my life for the first time. It wouldn't be the last. I cried on the floor to Coldplay and the man from Samaritans asked me if I could turn the light on. That was all. Just the light. I turned it on. It was all I had. And it was enough.

At 22, the worst heartbreak I'd ever felt hit me like a train. We had only been together for three months, but he felt like the one who would save me. Clinging onto that chance was everything to me. I cried on the floor to Coldplay until even my clothes were soaked with tears. I did it every day for six weeks.

At 23, I cupped in my hands the baby I had birthed at just ten weeks gestation. She would've been called Honour. I could see her little heart, dark through her translucent skin, and my world collapsed again. I cried on the floor to Coldplay. And then I cried on a Zoom full of people who had also lost babies, and there was this comforting echo of pain as I told them my story. I drunk wine out of a mug until I passed out.

There's something reassuring about hitting rock bottom. There's something reassuring about the fact I couldn't choose one event for this chapter. There are so many. Enough to fill a whole book. And yet, I'm still here. I'm not sure if there is anything in my life that I have more solid proof of than the fact that I can do all the hard things, and survive.

Isn't that incredible?

And here's more – rock bottom has produced my best art. My best writing. My best learning. My best revenge stories. Even if I couldn't see it at the time. There's a whole new level of the brain that gets accessed when you're in the dark: "Night Mode".

Night mode doesn't know what colours look like and what feelings feel like and how words sound, so it invents new ones. It doesn't understand structure and rules and living a certain way, so it lets you reinvent yourself so you can get through it. It takes you to the deepest darkest depths and holds you against your will until the very last breath of air is left in your lungs, and your whole entity evolves to keep you alive. You don't care what other people think, you're just trying to survive. You are being held hostage in the dark, and everything you thought you knew has changed. The world you thought you knew has changed.

So when you finally come back up for air..?

You get to start again.

*

At the time of writing this, I am two weeks fresh out of one of my darkest seasons on the back of a health diagnosis that has left me struggling to walk for weeks at a time. I spent six-months in the great depths of the dark, trying to comprehend how I was supposed to come to terms with permanently enduring this kind of chronic pain. I'd had to leave everything behind. My job as a yoga teacher, my financial security and my home. I moved back in with my family, miles away from the man I love, and I was drowning so intensely I really, truly didn't think I would survive it. And that is WITH my many, many previous experiences of Night Mode.

But we did it. Me and all the brave, resilient, enduring parts of the self. Fragmented from trauma but so great at working to keep me alive, separately and together.

My hair? Bright pink. We did it. I'm in the post-depression honeymoon phase but this one feels different. This one feels bigger. More real. I think I cracked open so hard I've found a treasure chest hidden within. I'm getting glimpses of 2020 Rebecca (we did it), and even further back, to a part of me I haven't properly met yet. She's wild, and fun, and at peace, and trusting. (We. Did. It).

This is the honeymoon "Alexa, play my End Credits playlist" phase. I'm pinching myself, shocked that I'm even still alive after such a long time underwater. I'm gathering all the items from the treasure chest, everything I found along that journey, all the missing pieces of the puzzle now lined up in a row and dazzling in the sun.

I am in the process of starting again, reinventing myself, discovering all the lost and forgotten parts of my soul that trauma took from me. I signed a soul contract to go into this deep murky dive (admittedly not knowing quite how awful it was going to be) and I found the treasure.

This experience was just another loss and crisis. As menial and ridiculously unimportant as it sounds. It will happen again. And again. And again. And I will survive it, again, and again and again.

I am beginning to learn that the peace within me doesn't seem to be particularly dependant on whether my life is 'right', but instead to do with how my psyche approaches things, after the initial insult and often lengthy processing phase anyway. I am still in physical pain but in a soul full of ecstasy. Financially poor but so internally rich. Emotionally hurting but healing like it's the air I need to breath, my ambrosia.

And it's the same with my previous deep dives – I am still grieving my losses, the violence, the trauma. Life isn't suddenly fine when the major issues aren't in the forefront anymore. I am simply more gracious with my feelings towards them. I no longer blame myself. I take the time to work through feelings rather than shut them away. I don't see 'low days' as failures but as necessary healing that need my time and understanding.

And sometimes, these experiences will need a lot of unpacking. They may not leave us with grace and light but instead with PTSD, debilitating trust issues or life changing circumstances. The process of reinventing ourselves might just be the hardest part. Asking for help, and committing to it, can be equally as challenging.

We must take a moment to grieve all that was lost. The opportunities missed, relationships broken or changed, pain so emotionally consuming it was hard to move most days. And following that, we must take a moment to feel proud of ourselves for the tremendous strength and resilience we conjured up seemingly from nowhere. I know you didn't want to, who wants to be strong all the time? But you did it nevertheless. For you. For your soul. For the process. For the learning. For the hope. You should be so proud.

There will be people who never understand loss and crisis in the way you and I do. Who never truly know what the dark feels like. And yes, they are lucky, but so are we. We have this unique level of understanding and transformation that truly is a superpower. We need their naivety to remind us not to take things too seriously. We need our depth to remind us that we can hold pain and that others can hold pain, without letting it burn them to a crisp.

I am so very sorry for all the horrible things you have had to endure. But I am so very proud of you that you did.

LESSON 15: FOR FIVE MINUTES

Compassion with a capital C is the only way through The Darkness. If you're in it right now, you can bet I'd be dishing out one of the following quotes to you:

"One breath at a time"

"One second at a time"

"One minute at a time"

"One day at a time"

(Depending on what you need). And even though you can sense this compassion, you'll still have the people around you who don't get it, who are wondering why your work performance is slipping, or why you haven't walked the dog in a week, or why you aren't calling your grandparents enough. Even if you explain to them that you are in The Dark, you are living in Night Mode, they will still question where last week's assignment is.

This behaviour is to be expected. We can name them Night Mode Gremlins. Their mission is to try and break you, to try and stop you from finding the compassionate torch of light you need to get you through. It's not personal. If they knew how much pain you were in, they wouldn't dare. But they don't and probably never will, no matter how much you try and explain, so they dare.

Your job here is to somehow find it in you to ignore the outcries of society telling you you're failing. Is to ignore your sociopathic boss asking you to work more hour's even though your daughter has just died.

Right now, none of that matters. For you are in The Dark. And the only thing that matters in the dark is surviving.

When life is battering you like a sea storm to sandstone, you have to access the contingency plan of functioning and existence. This means lowering your expectations of what you hope to achieve and how you run your life, just temporarily. You have to start treating yourself like you would do your five-year-old self, stood crying in front of you, having been through everything you have, feeling everything you do. Ask her what SHE needs right now, a five-year-old, with all of that pain. A bath? A nap? Chocolate and Netflix? A bear hug? This isn't laziness, but survival and recovery. Keep reminding yourself of that.

I highly recommend 'chunking down' both your thought processes and your daily tasks. Non-essential tasks can all go on hold for now. For essential tasks, perhaps start by aiming for five minutes, or even one if that feels too much. For example, if you need to walk the dog but that seems far too daunting, just do it for five minutes. Even if that only means you've walked round the corner and back, or across the road. Need a wash? Spend five minutes with baby wipes, or washing in the sink. Food? Get ready meals that don't take more than five minutes to prepare.

And if you have bigger projects to sort, like washing the clothes or cleaning the house, work with five minutes at a time. Spend five minutes sorting the clothes that need washing. Then, take a break, as much time as you need, it could even be the next day. The next five minutes of energy can be spent loading them into the machine. Then we break again. And so on, and so on. You'll often find that the simple act of taking the pressure away from yourself to 'get everything done now or else' will be enough to find the energy to do it. Other times, one minutes devotion of energy can feel impossible. Either way, you are doing these with compassion for yourself, not judgement.

There will be some situations where you have no choice but to carry on. Parents for example, or carers. At this point, where possible, we outsource. We ask for help. (Even just for five minutes). If you have the finances or family and friend resources, you can outsource things like house chores, cooking meals, pick-ups and drop offs and even emotional support. If you don't have those options, you work with one-breath-at-a-time increments. And keep reminding yourself with as much compassion as you can source that one day this will pass.

During loss and crisis you have got to get good at saying no. "No I can't do that this week", "No, I'm not able to at the moment" and my personal favourite: "I don't have capacity right now". If you've been waiting for a chance to learn how to set boundaries, now's the time. Night Mode will let you be ruthless, it will give you that power and that confidence. Lean into that and it will lead you to the light.

And if you start feeling guilty for any of the techniques you have to implement during this time, keep reminding yourself that this is temporary. This is you showing kindness and compassion to yourself when you need it most. This is you putting your mask on first and modelling to others around you that this is what we do when shit hits the fan.

One breath at a time.

LESSON 16: DEATH IS FOR THE LIVING

Some of the darkest, most beautiful pain we will know here is grief. All of us, at some point in our lives, will know grief. You might meet several times. You might meet so many times it feels like it will never leave. Sometimes it doesn't. And that's okay too.

Knowing grief is knowing love. And I fucking hate that saying whilst being in a relationship with it at the same time.

Grief is the outpouring of a loss of love – which means that *you* got to know what it was. Whether that's through heartbreak or the death of a loved one or even an opportunity that's no longer there. Grief is real and valid and pure. And grief says that we have tried for something. We have given ourselves, our time, our hearts, simply for the sake of it. Simply for love and hope and joy. It's a remarkable reminder that love lives here. It is one of the most powerful feelings in the world.

Sometimes grief is complicated. Intertwined with unanswered questions and painful truths that make it hard to feel grief in the way we're supposed to. Sometimes it seems to drift away too quickly, only to bounce back years later from a stranger's perfume or a loose ceiling tile that reminds you of them (don't ask).

Sometimes we begin grieving whilst someone is still alive. Anticipatory grief feels secret and illegal. "This isn't about me!" you tell yourself.

"It's them who is dying..."

Yet it's you who is left.

It's you who watches helplessly as they leave without you. As they suffer and fade. Grief isn't about them. Grief is about you. (Although the grief of dying itself is a whole different treacherous experience). Grief is about what you lose, which can be anything from a good friend to your sense of security to someone who makes your responsibilities less intense. Grief is because you will miss them. You will lose them. You might suffer and fade helplessly without them.

Grief is selfish. And I'm so here for it.

Grief is for everyone. The dying and the thriving, the young and the old. Grief is the process within ourselves as we journey through the separation process from someone or something we had developed an attachment to.

Death on the other hand is quick and fast and done. Dying can be slow and tragic and painful.

Grief is the beautiful reminder that we did it, we connected. We felt. We shared. We knew. And the rather humbling one that we can lose it all in an instant. And the only thing left at the end of it all...is you.

For the grief that lives with us – and I assure you, there are many of us who walk around daily with her sitting on our shoulders – we have to find a way to keep going, even as she weighs us down.

In one of grief's very painful visits to me, injustice and anger was pulsing through my body. For weeks I only saw red, rage eating me up inside. It wasn't fair. It was too soon. Too young. Too cruel.

She was so special. So special that I knew no one would ever know her the way I did. And that was it.

No one will ever know how lucky I was to have her for the time I did. No one will know the joy she brought me, the light she showed me. No one will know the love I was exposed to, that I didn't even know existed. Except me. And what a gift that was!

I had stepped through the wardrobe and been to Narnia. I got to share my precious time on this earth with the kind of soul that many people may never meet in this lifetime. I got that – little old ME got that experience. How blessed I was to have felt love so deeply, to have known light so strong.

She gave me the power to believe that there is something bigger than who we are. A love more powerful than we even know. And my goodness do we have a huge capacity to feel it all should we let ourselves.

And even though my trip to Narnia was short-lived, it happened. I got to go there, I got to witness her beauty, I got to be changed by her presence in my life. And I knew that one day it would outweigh the heartbreak I felt in those moments.

I was given the gift of Narnia, and for that, I wouldn't change a single second. There is no guarantee that I get to go back to Narnia. But if there's one thing we must take from Aslan's words: things never happen the same way twice.

Several years later, I lost a baby. A couple of days before my miscarriage I had one of the most intense dreams of my life. According to the doctors, baby had only died a couple of days prior, so I like to think it was a message from baby to me as she passed over.

I had been adamant from the beginning that she was a girl. Adamant. And perhaps in human form she was. But in this dream, there was a baby boy involved:

I was in the middle of nowhere, in a field next to a petrol station, and there was a young lady who had just had a baby boy. She was careless and naïve, and hiding from her abusive ex, who was coming after us in this dream. I volunteered to take the baby and transport it to another realm where it would be safe until she was able and ready to get it.

She passed the baby to me, and I held it in my arms. For many days after this dream I relived the feeling of his tiny body against mine. I could truly feel the temperature of his skin. I could feel how much he weighed. What he smelt like. I watched his tiny little face scrunch up and release as little noises came from his mouth.

It felt so real. Even when I was awake. It felt as real as it did being pregnant. It was only when I spoke of this dream out loud after I had miscarried that I realised what this message was.

This wasn't my baby to keep, it was mine to protect and carry and transport to another realm. This baby wasn't meant to come earth side. I had done someone a favour. I had been a hero. I did the job I had set out to do. I didn't fail at all.

It's given me so much comfort thinking this way. Finding spiritual meaning in loss gives me so much peace. And I showed myself a part of me I never knew existed: selflessness. A complete and utter dedication to another being, regardless of the impacts it had on me. Even I surprised myself.

I want you to feel grief unapologetically. I want you to let it ravish your flesh with no mercy, if that's what feels right. I want you to wear black if you want to wear black, even if everyone else is in bright colours by now.

Trust your body to guide you through this transition. Ask for help when you need it. Take time off if that is what will help. Do not dismiss your grief even if you feel like you shouldn't be feeling it this way. It is important to *you*, and that's what matters.

It can be easy for people to want to jump to 'a celebration of life' before the inner experience of death has even begun to process itself.

Death is for the living and this grief is about you. And you're allowed to feel that, even if everyone else is doing it a different way (and they will be, we all grieve differently).

Honour the process of detachment, however that looks for you.

LESSON 17: REGULATION STATION

In long types of crisis, particularly mental health related ones, we will often try multiple times to get ourselves out of it. It's uncomfortable. We don't want to be in it. We want to survive. We want to thrive. We want to live again. Little do we know that there is no quick fix out.

Sometimes attitude and behaviour changes DO make a difference and DO impact the end-date. And sometimes, no matter how hard we try, we are meant to be in the dark for a little longer still. Surrendering to that is heartbreaking but beautiful.

When it's really painful, I'll do all the things. I'll drink all the water and join the gym and do the gut reset and start journalling and read affirmations out loud twenty times a day because people rave about it and how it will 'fix me in two weeks'.

"Here I am, slumped on the kitchen floor throwing affirmations at the wall until one sticks. I twirl the soggy spaghetti pieces of abundance and manifestations around my fingers, I even wear them as a moustache on my face. But still. No luck. What might it take to become more than my own limitations?" - I journal. I'm doing everything right, right?

When it's really painful, I'll pop self-help books like pills. Chucking them back with a swig of distilled-flouride-free-because-someone-somewhere-said-so-water. I'll write notes on them as if I'm doing a university assignment, desperate to grasp it all because Surely Then It Will Fix Me.

Occasionally the Hypochondriac within will decide that these heavy feelings must be caused by a vitamin deficiency, or a brain tumour or hormonal abnormalities. It will convince me that I just need to take some 'ancient natural healing Bush grass' or 'hand-plucked from a rare plant that has just been discovered vegan Vitamin D that I saw on Instagram' to fix. (Anything other than committing to therapy I swear).

I'll see chakra healers and psychics and magic medicine women and God but THE PAIN IS STILL THERE. Sometimes I will do anything not to Sit With It and the Universe will do everything to make me.

So, when I eventually do surrender to feeling it all and choose to live through the experience in order to receive the beauty (like a six-month long tattoo), I need short term management solutions so that I don't completely lose it.

(And listen, sometimes you will completely lose it and smash things up and impulsively sell your car on a whim and then walk three miles home and realise you literally can't get around anymore because you're too rural and now you might not see anyone for months at a time and will they even deliver food here or are you going to starve to death and you've actually just made things so much worse. Sometimes it just will happen. It's okay. You find your way eventually.)

This is where I created the regulation station. I've learnt that for me, my moments of panic and desperation and 'I need to do something right now or I might die' are actually because my nervous system is so dysregulated, so triggered from faulty childhood learning, that it really does think I am in a life or death situation and I need to get out of it right now.

It's more than just in my head – it's in my body too. It is somatic.

Our bodies are designed to protect us, not to make us happy. Sometimes the pain is so great that your body tells you the only way to make it stop is to die. It is simply craving safety.

I keep my regulation station close by at all times. The notes app on your phone, or a journal you take everywhere with you are good options. It looks pretty and reminds me of me. I've doodled flowers and peaceful greens all over it. (Colour psychology is another topic I've explored and blamed for all my problems all in one).

It's a list of 'instant reset' options to try out when I am in crisis. Short and quick options to get me out of immediate danger.

Your list will look different to mine, but here's a start:

REGULATION STATION

-Deep and slow diaphragmatic breathing.

-Lie on the floor.

-Single nostril breathing.

-Squeeze your feet (this is my body's safe place and helps me feel grounded – yours might be different).

-Stretch, like slow flow yoga but not so serious.

-Chamomile tea, double teabag it.

-[Insert emergency prescription sedative medication here if that works for you].

-[Insert emergency natural medication here if that works for you]

-Paint shells (this is a cute therapeutic hobby of mine, colouring is also a good one).

-Move legs as if they are running (letting the body think you ARE running from the danger, other somatic options are 'stomping' on the spot or intuitive dance).

-Go for a walk.

-Get in some water, or simply run your hands through it.

-Dextrous tasks that distract your mind such as knitting, origami or pottery.

-Write, write, write.

-Rewatch my old YouTube videos (which both reminds me that 'strong me' does exist, and also 'I have done hard things before' me has survived them).

-Find something that smells comforting and hold it close.

-Wrap your body up nice and tightly in something warm like a blanket or dressing gown – it's a self-hug!

-Sing or scream the tension out of your body.

-Call someone you know will hold you with their words.

The purpose of the regulation station is to help ground your nervous system when it is getting a little too wild. It is calm you telling not-calm you what to do, which is possibly exactly what you need in that moment.

You'll know when you need it, and you'll learn that you already knew what to do. You know yourself best, and coming home to this list in times of crisis will be the reassuring reminder of that.

Let's get regulating.

REGULATION STATION

- _____
- _____
- _____
- _____
- _____
- _____
- _____
- _____
- _____
- _____
- _____
- _____

LESSON 18: TO LOVE AND LET GO

Occasionally when one lives in the dark long enough, you will catch glimpses of shooting stars, meteors. You think to yourself: 'Finally, it's the end, the light is coming. If I hold onto this hard enough it will fill up the sky with light too!'. Now, I must tell you something, a public service announcement if you like...

If you hold onto a meteor whilst it is blazing through the sky shooting glorious colours through the dark, you will be in rather immense pain. The heat'll get ya, for one. But more than that, the longing will.

Feeling joy in Night Mode is a good sign. You're noticing things again. Seeing things differently. It can feel like a huge, immense relief. You remember what it feels like to have warmth on your skin, and blood in your heart. It can feel like that huge gulp of air you take after being underwater for the longest time.

But alas, it was not to stay. It feels like a cruel trick on your psyche. It feels like betrayal in the worst form, taunting and teasing you, poking you in the dark. In a panic, you reach out and grab it, hands bloody as it tries aggressively to escape. You hold on still, and now your body is being shaken up, bruised, battered, bleeding as the light cries out to you "You must let go!".

But it is impossible. You've been in the dark for so long that you deserve this light. This is YOUR light. And you want it all back now. You can't let go. If you let go it would look like you weren't trying hard enough. If you let go you might never see the light again, you might even forget what it looks like.

If you love something, let it go.

Light, and love for that matter, cannot be manufactured. They cannot be whipped up with a handful of magic ingredients, the right time and temperature. They can look like they can. Very convincingly so in fact. But it is merely a façade, a mask.

That job will make me feel better. A boyfriend will make me feel better. A dog. A hundred thousand. That pill. This dress. That holiday. Travelling the world. If I just hold onto that version of me. That weekend away. That experience. That person that's no longer with us, that will make me feel better.

Yeah, it will. For a while. And there might just be precious moments of those memories that etch themselves into your soul forever. You lucky thing.

You might make your entire identity about that light. So afraid of it slipping away from you that it must be the only thing you ever talk about. But don't you see? If you're having to grip onto something that tightly, then perhaps it was never truly yours in the first place? Perhaps nothing is? And perhaps that's exactly how it's meant to be.

And I do want you to feel it all – that love is so beautiful and delicate when it does come. Feel it all. Feel the light. Feel that joy as it finally washes over you after such a long drought. Let it all soak in. Whilst knowing it is not yours to keep. It is not here to stay, and that this is all part of the process of walking back into the light.

Here's what happens if you let go of the good stuff, the good memories, the good 'versions of you' (hint hint, wink wink, you know what I'm talking about here right? #2020rebecca).

You let brand new opportunities in. New joy. New light. New love. New life. New memories. New moments. With no expectations of how they're supposed to be or what they're supposed to feel like.

Surrendering to this experience and embracing the way joy shows up in different ways...gah, it's pretty miraculous really. If you can trust that life will yet again bring you some joy, some love and light, peace and happiness, in whatever way IT sees fit - then it will come back to you.

Don't you see that as you open your arms wide to let it all go, you're creating space to bring even more back in?

Don't you see that in trusting so fully that you can survive this darkness that you are fast-tracking your way out?

Don't you see that the process of loving and letting go is exactly what this experience came to teach you in the first place?

These little shooting stars have not come to taunt you, but to remind you to keep holding on. They have come as a sign to guide you towards the light – alone, but with hope.

It is the trust that does it. The never-ending unquestionable faith that precedes it. It takes courage, but boy does it feel good to love and let things go.

Even the good things.

LESSON 19: YOU ARE SO MUCH MORE THAN HOW YOU THINK ABOUT YOURSELF WHEN YOU'RE AFRAID

Loss and crisis will instil fear into the best of us. Suddenly, everything we knew is gone, and nothing feels safe anymore. Suddenly life seems fleeting and we feel tiny and out of control. Some of us live in fear our whole lives. Some of us have been stuck in a loss and crisis cycle that seems impossible to escape. So impossible in fact that we let it become part of us, who we are. "Oh I'm used to it" you'll say, or "This happens to me a lot". "It's just the way things are."

Sometimes we live our lives smaller than we actually are, because that was the safest way to navigate our childhoods, which our body still thinks we are living in. It was unsafe as a child to have strengths, or be successful, or be yourself, so you end up restricting your potential as an adult because that's what your body thinks will keep you alive.

"I'm just the fat one/quiet one/lazy one/loud one/can't hold down a job one/too independent for a relationship one, you don't need to worry about me, (I'm not a threat, please don't hurt me)".

When you are living in fear there isn't time to feel good about yourself. The focus is survival, not satisfactory relationships with the mind and body. The focus is people pleasing, and keeping everybody sweet, all the time. Not boundaries and self-respect. The focus is staying quiet, small, insignificant, not honouring the beautiful essence of what it means to be YOU.

Can you imagine who you would be without the fear?

Can you imagine all the things you would do if you weren't afraid?

Can you imagine how you would feel about yourself if it wasn't dominated by fear-based insecurities?

Because here's the deep truth that you need to take a second to breath in right now: You are so much more than how you think about yourself when you're afraid. Monumentally so in fact. You are inspiring. You are honest and true. You are confident and you take up the space and it is wonderful. You have the capacity to be so much more than what the world has taught you that you can be. Without fear you are a fucking diamond.

And sometimes, seeing ourselves without those protective shells can be a little too much.

Who am I without the depression? Who am I without the volatile relationships? What am I worth if everyone isn't validating me all the time?

You are human.

You are messy.

You are learning.

And you have shadows hiding underneath that will want some attention too. Taking off the mask isn't pretty at first. We have to face parts of ourselves that we don't like so much. And I don't just mean the fear-based parts. I mean the narcissistic habits. I mean acknowledging how we've hurt people. Accessing the guilt we've buried underneath. There's lots to unpack and you've got to be ready and prepared to do that. To be humbled, and within that, find the truth of yourself.

Many people spend their whole lives summoning up the courage to get to that point.

But you don't have to.

You are so much more than how you think about yourself when you're afraid; the good, the bad, the ugly and the goddamn beautiful.

Stop holding yourself back because you're scared of what you might uncover. The authenticity of embracing it all makes it all worth it in the end. I swear.

YOU ARE SO MUCH MORE THAN HOW YOU THINK about YOURSELF WHEN YOU'RE AFRAID

LESSON 20: YOU'LL FIND THE CHAOS IF THAT'S WHAT YOU BELIEVE IN

It's rather torturous of me to turn on you now with this rather rude lesson, dear ones. But I couldn't avoid it either.

There's a difference between heightened self-awareness and self-obsession. Trust me, I would know, I am the CEO of self-obsession. It comes from wondrous intentions. 'I will heal myself'. And thus - 'I will be of greater benefit to the world around me and the people in my life'.

But those intentions, like any obsessive hobby (I'm bizarrely thinking of both trainspotters and base jumpers here) can become misguided. 'I will heal myself' becomes 'I will find all the chaos within me and just get lost in it until I figure my shit out'. Which becomes 'I fucking love the chaos, I ain't leaving now, this feels safe'.

We become chaos worshippers. Addicted to the high of finding out new problems with ourselves and watching them unfold in front of us as we frantically take notes. 'This relationship will be no good for me, but I'm fascinated to see how I handle it!', for example. 'Having a chaotic life makes me edgy, I'm so much more now than just quiet Betty from down the street, I AM CHAOS AND I LOVE CHAOS AND CHAOS IS ME', as another.

Similarly: 'Who am I without the drama?"

Once you get out of chronic trauma that may have gone on for years, stillness, peace and calm, kind relationships and 'nothing going wrong' can feel very, very wrong. If you grew up on edge all the time, that was your normal, that was your safety. How can you possibly expect yourself to feel comfortable when nothing is wrong after all those years of living a certain way? It is by no means an instant or easy fix. An instant or easy learning.

I challenge you now to ask yourself about the relationships you have in your life, such as friends and lovers.

Do they represent calm or chaos?

Ask yourself about your work, spending time with family, or your social life.

Chaos? Or Calm?

And if they are chaotic, do you keep choosing them anyway? Isn't that what you believe in? Isn't that how life is meant to be? Don't you get a kick out of the exhaustion and frustration of it all, somewhere deep down?

(Isn't that what you were taught safety meant?)

There was a time in my life where I had six jobs on the trot. I worked 16-hour days and didn't believe in weekends or holidays. Sleep was for the weak and leisure time was just finding more ways to build my businesses and get better at my jobs. People around me were in awe of my drive. But really? It was never going to be enough for me. I always needed to work harder, longer, faster, make more sacrifices, cross more of my own boundaries.

I was so addicted to being the 'boss bitch who doesn't stop' that I was willing to surrender my own dignity and health to make sure I could get the chaos kick. I was unstoppable, and equally self-destructive.

And then Covid came, and six jobs and small businesses ventures whittled rapidly down to one.

I was playing music all day and all night just so that I wasn't left alone with my thoughts.

I was newly single, for the first time in my adult life. And I had no idea what to do outside of the chaotic masterpiece I had been living in. I loved the chaos, didn't I? I needed to get it back, didn't I?

I swapped chaos for countryside. I walked and walked and walked. I took my shoes off and squeezed my toes into the muddy gorgeous earth and began to truly see myself for the first time.

Without the chaos I had been forced to feel all the feelings I'd shut away for so long (and fuck me the tsunami of that was pretty tough at first). But I also realised how cool I am WITHOUT the chaos. And that actually, I don't want the chaos anymore.

I want a peaceful life. And I want to curate my life so that it gives me the time and space to heal from all the painful things I've experienced, whilst learning to love and trust and integrate into the world as a traumatised human all at the same time.

You will find the chaos if that's what you believe in. And sometimes, it feels so believable we consider it fact. 'Oh, I just like to be busy!' Do you? Or do you keep busy so it fills the void and stops you from having to access your feelings? (Insert *Mic drop* here).

Do you keep busy because it reminds you of your chaotic childhood and a part of you craves the false sense of security that gave you before you had your own adult responsibilities? (*Smashes mic through window*).

Do you keep busy because you actually have no idea who you are outside of that and getting to know yourself at this point in your life and recognizing how many mistakes you've made by living inauthentically terrifies you? (*Smashes mic through window and turns into a firework that vibrates so loudly random car alarms go off and dogs start barking).

Being in chaos addiction recovery isn't easy, and slipping into old patterns does happen from time to time (or sometimes they manifest in different ways, like excessive exercising for example). But once you've begun to see who you are outside of constantly being busy, you're on the right tracks for a real adventure: loving yourself.

PART 4: DATING YOURSELF

When I think back to the person I was before I learnt to love myself, I don't recognise her. Through some wonderful internal nudge, I have been documenting my life experiences either on the internet or through journalling and songwriting long before 2020. And rather than seeing these videos and blogs of myself and feeling shame or anger, I am filled with compassion at all the things I survived, and all the ways I moulded myself to keep myself safe.

Critical moments of change often come after breakups or losses, (or even hair dying episodes). But the changes that came for me in 2020 were not simply about radical self-acceptance, but about getting to know myself in the first place. I had absolutely no idea who I was, what I liked, what was important to me, what I wanted to achieve. All I had known was survival and chasing highs.

I remember the exact moment I saw myself for the first time. I was walking my dog Skye on one of my 'four milers' amongst the stunning Cornish coastal countryside, my Covid retreat and family home. It was April, we were in the thick of lockdown. Everyone was terrified about their jobs, their health, the future, the world as we knew it.

And I took my shoes off and started dancing. In the middle of nowhere with music playing out from my phone. We had a Springtime weather forecast none of us will ever forget, and the sun beamed down on me as I threw my hands in the air, it was cheering me on.

The joy bubbled up from such a deep place within me that I started laughing uncontrollably, kicking my legs out and pulling faces at my dog, who thought we were playing a game.

Anyone could have walked by at any point – something that would usually be a massive problem (what would they think of me?), but it hadn't even crossed my mind. And I couldn't believe I felt like this. I couldn't believe the spirit inside me had the confidence to burst out so deliciously like she had in this moment.

I, for the first time, loved myself.

'Dancing walks' slowly became a regular thing, and people did see me, which made them smile, and made me smile too. Sometimes I would take a book with me, or some lunch, and just soak in the Cornish air, or go for a swim in the glistening waves – running out as fast as I ran in, screaming delightfully as the cold made me squirm.

I found myself laughing at my silliness, my accidents, my mistakes, rather than criticising and shaming myself. I started the 'Getting To Know Myself List' and began to want to find out every little thing about who I was as person. I wanted to love myself. I wanted to be so in love with myself that nothing and no one could ever take away the strength and safety I was cultivating within.

Restrictions began to lift, and I took things up a notch. I'd gone from dating to 'going steady' with myself. I went out on long hikes and picnics, to aquariums and theme parks, National Trusts and cinemas, cafes and restaurants, all by myself. It's the most liberating thing I've ever done.

You think that everybody is looking at you, you think that everybody must be pitying you and talking about your solo-ness to their friends and partners, but literally no-one is. And in fact, lots of people out there are on their own adventures too! And once you get used to it, you stop caring anyway. You're so in love with this amazing spirit within you that other people's opinions don't phase you.

When you love yourself like that, handling the tough times feels easier too. You feel like a naked solo full moon dance in the rain to clear your energy? Cool, let's do it. Want to go on a long drive into the countryside and just find a random field where you can lie in the grass and watch the clouds as you sob through the heaviness and talk to yourself? Couldn't think of anything better mate.

And don't get me started on the dance parties I had in my living room. Or the photoshoots where I'd take a suitcase down to the beach full of fun outfits to try on, to the horror of dog walkers as I'd accidentally flash them as I got changed. Or the nights where I couldn't sleep but it didn't matter, I'd write instead, or play guitar, or the keyboard I'd decided to acquire even though I didn't know how to play.

I started finding out the things I loved and wanted to learn more about them, LET myself learn more about them. I qualified as an astrologer, dived into Shakespeare and became a fangirl for The 1975 and Taylor Swift (I know, I know). I learnt photography, and how to cook exciting dishes and how to do DIY. I redecorated my house and built flatpack furniture and wallpapered all by myself.

Self-pleasure, in every element, was invited into my life. From solo orgasms to orgasmic luxury dinners. Duvet days and movie nights to solo travelling to Greece and making new friends just through this newfound magnetism and radiance that glowed when I learnt how to love myself.

It was, and always will be, the best relationship I've ever had. And it was with myself.

*

So where did it all go wrong? (You can see why it bothered me so much now, right?)

I've blamed everything from the changing of the planetary alignments to the self-abandonment that occurs in a new relationship to restrictions lifting to a black cat crossing my path in the street.

I spent more time trying to find a cause than I did trying to get back there. I needed something to blame other than 'I just got too comfortable and stopped putting the effort in'. Because the end results were too cataclysmic for it to 'just' be that.

How could I betray myself and slip back into toxic thought patterns so easily? Whilst knowing with every cell in my body how good it felt to love myself the way I did?

Facing my own negative traits and being willing to change and approach myself head on was a pretty intense experience. Instead of dating myself, I started hating myself, my inner voice acting like a disgruntled ex-lover by slagging me off to everyone I knew. Self-sabotage became an addiction, and I ended up hauling myself 300 miles away from everyone I loved, selling my car and quite literally enforcing self-isolation.

At the beginning, there was a peace. I was back in nature and by the sea and for my body the ocean is like coming back home. At first, I medicated, as I had been for many moons. I had an entire suitcase full of medication in fact. Through (what I call) the wonders of the ocean air, and perhaps a little bit of magic, one month later I was off all medication. Completely and entirely. For the first time in years.

Then I masturbated like a pubescent teenager who had just discovered the WooHoo button on Sims2. Day in and day out it was my fixation. It got me through the day, a mood boosting medication in a far more physical form. Maybe it was just a distraction, a toxic addiction distracting me from my truth. Or maybe my body was crying out for connection, a desperate yearning for me to See Her As She Is and listen to what she was trying to tell me. "Look how much pleasure is within you!" she would cry. "Look how much we could give to each other if you just let me in!"

And then I started to meditate. At first it just pissed me off. It was so hard to sit still and not plague my mind with awful words about myself. But after a while, a huge feeling of surrender washed over my soul. "Okay. Fuck it. Let's feel it all. Let's deal with this beef we've got going on. Let's have it all out until there's nothing left to say, go on."

And there was so much I had to say. So much guilt and resent and shame and anger and bitterness. So much frustration and hatred and disappointment and fear. I was in mediation with my mind for months.

But slowly, through journalling and remembering how to dance and watching so many episodes of The Crown that I started talking to myself in their accents, the mediating businessmen in my brain took off their suits and lay naked next to each other, staring up at the stars.

"Maybe it's not about getting back there, to 2020?" The mind said, as the night breeze whispered through the nooks and folds in his skin.

"Or maybe it was just a taster of what we have the potential to achieve?" The soul added.

"Maybe loving ourself looks different now? So much has changed since that year, how can we expect ourselves to just bounce back to the way things were before? Maybe that's too much?" The mind looked over to the soul with curiosity instead of resistance for the first time.

"Maybe you're right. Maybe we have to find a new way to do life? I think we could start by not fighting anymore... I'm exhausted, aren't you?" The soul sighed.

"Completely and utterly" they both laughed. "Truce?"

"Truce".

Medication. Masturbation. Meditation.

Returning to the home within my soul to allow all the parts of myself to work together.

The businessmen in my brain had a long way to go, but they wore yoga pants now and scrapped the ties. Workplace dance sessions were made compulsory, and the team were offered weekly therapy sessions that they had to commit to for a minimum of six months. They had a long way to go before things would feel a little easier, but the protocols were set in place for changes to be made, together, as one.

LESSON 21: THE LITTLE WAYS YOU LOVE YOURSELF

So, this is where we begin the journey of falling in love with ourselves. Perhaps for the first time ever. And we're working in baby steps. Breath by breath, second by second.

But here's the plot twist: you're already doing it.

I know, I rolled my eyes when I wrote that too.

But hear me out. You are already performing tiny acts of love to yourself without even realising. They look like self-care, self-nurture, forward thinking messengers of hope. Or, as you might currently perceive them: mundane tasks you have to do as part of being human.

Here's some examples:

-Taking a deep breath. (Gah that's so loving).

-Getting out of bed in the morning. Or to go for a pee in the night. That was kind.

-Washing.

-Dressing.

-Eating (we call it 'nourishing' ourselves now, this is your memo).

-Humming to yourself because it feels comforting and gentle.

-Smiling to yourself because you thought of something funny, or happy.

-Dancing in the car because your favourite tune came on and your body said 'YES'.

-Choosing a drink you prefer, because you like it, and you deserve the things you like.

-Having favourites of anything - you're honouring what you like. (Are you getting it yet?)

- Saving the Yorkshire pudding as the last part of your roast dinner, because you know you like it best and it's something to be excited for.

-Putting comfy clothes on when you get in the house.

-[Consensually] petting a stranger's dog, because it brings you joy, and you deserve that.

Are you seeing it? The ways that you are choosing love – self-love – without even realising it? It's more than 'well that's just being a human', you are pro-joy, and don't even know it. You are subconsciously putting some effort into that relationship with yourself without even thinking about it.

You're doing it!

But that's not all. Now that you know the secret (that you do love and care and want well for yourself underneath the façade of self-sabotage and self-dismissal) you can do it MORE. You can begin to actively choose the little ways to make your life a little more comfortable, easier, joyful, light. Whatever feels safe for you to call it right now. (I know that admitting you deserve happiness and peace can be challenging for those of us used to beating ourselves up, so find your own way of describing the journey here).

You can begin – slowly and breath by breath – to honour the things that feel good *for you*. And to steer away from the things that don't. We're only talking about the small stuff right now, (let's pace ourselves here folks we've got a whole book to get through yet).

And those little, tiny baby changes could look like:

-Actually, I really don't like the taste of Gin, and I'm going to ask for something else next time even though everyone else is drinking that.

-I am going to sit in bed and watch TV tonight because I know that's what I need right now, even though everyone else tells me it's unproductive and bad for me.

-I love wearing tight clothes and crop tops even if they're 'so 2010' and they don't make me look the way society expects me to, they make *me* feel good and that is what's important.

- Actually, I love/hate getting up early, and am going to see if I can adjust my work schedule to fit that so I can utilise my best hours and ensure I am respecting my own energy.

And you know what this is? It's more than just 'making life a bit easier', you are opening the doors to a relationship with the best person you will ever meet. You are giving yourself permission for that to begin. You are showing the universe, the world and all the people in it where you have the capacity to feel love. Even in small ways.

Especially in small ways.

YOU ARE THE LOVE YOU HAVE BEEN LOOKING FOR

LESSON 22: THE GETTING TO KNOW YOURSELF LIST

The funny thing about dating yourself for the first time is that you have to get to know yourself from SCRATCH. Like 'all I know about this person is that they are holding a fish in their profile photo' scratch. And this is probably something you've never thought of before. You probably think you already know yourself. There's nothing more to learn, so why should I ask, why should I try and get to know myself better when I already do?

You might think you know yourself. You know your favourite colour, the kind of food you like or what your favourite dog breed is. But do you notice the quirky little habits you have that you only ever notice in somebody else? Like how you always fold up a crisp packet into crispogami after you're finished? Or how you speak to ladybugs the same way you would a dog? Or the expressions you make on your face when you see something peculiar in public (Jim Halpert where you at?).

Do you know the things that make your heart sing, truly, deeply. Do you know why Bridgerton series make you so happy or why you cry with joy every time you see a stranger's wedding taking place and clap and giggle on the spot even though it's kinda weird because you weren't invited?

Do you know what you don't like? (And no, not just mushrooms or leather trousers). But the smell of freshly laid tar, or when it rains and everyone gets dramatic and acts like it's going to burn their skin rather than just embracing getting a bit soggy. Or how annoying you find those annoying 10-page long acknowledgment sections at the beginning of a book you can't wait to get your teeth into, and you're desperate to skip past it but you feel like you have to read every single part of it in case there are any hidden secrets in amongst the AND I MUST THANK...essays to people you've never even heard of.

The Getting To Know Yourself list should be a prerequisite to dating anybody else. How can you possibly expect anybody else to see and know you for who you are if you cannot see you yourself? (And even more so than that, if my records are correct, beginning this journey and creating this list will make you enjoy dating yourself so much, you won't be that fussed about dating anyone else, which is EXACTLY how you want to approach relationships – more on that later).

Let today be the first day of a friendship that will truly last a lifetime, go and open up your notes app. And for reference (and a full willingness to humiliate myself in public) here is mine.

Getting To Know Me

- I like to let the credits run a little at the end of a movie before I leave to let the film sink in.
- I always sniff milk before I pour it.
- My belly button is a no touch area.
- I believe jewellery creates a field around you when you wear it depending on who/what it's associated with.
- I am a "critical observer" meaning I notice very small changes about myself and my environment.
- I am extremely sensitive to smell and taste.
- I find an Irish accent attractive.
- I think about having a baby every single day and have done since I was 15.

- I think about Thailand most days.

- I like thunderstorms, I used to have an extreme phobia of them and had to have hypnotherapy for it.

- I can be extremely impulsive and unpredictable.

- In the past I didn't know my emotional boundaries and ended up putting myself in situations where I got hurt/had lasting damage and trauma.

- I hate seeing my brown roots it reminds me of when I had depression.

- I'm actually very anxious about snow.

- I love Scouting for Girls, Leddra chapman, Taylor Swift, Coldplay, The 1975, The Weeknd, Jeremy Zucker.

-Astrological compatibility is a deal breaker for me. UPDATE: was. It's on my mind. I'm trying to be more open minded about it.

-I like Joni Mitchell.

-One of my favourite words is Butterscotch.

-I bite my thumb when I'm anxious.

-I HATE mushrooms. Update: I'm trying to add them to my food because they're *healthy*.

-I still hate spicy food.

-I like spontaneity but I prefer planning.

-I DIG hand tattoos/male hands in general.

-I love learning the meaning of new words (the descriptive ones).

-I still don't know the difference between nouns and verbs and adjectives and all that. Very confusing.

-I would drink and breathe Shakespeare if I could.

-Twelfth night is the best Shakespeare.

-I know Orsino's soliloquy 'If Music Be the Food of Love' off by heart and sometime say it out loud when I'm in a romantic setting and pretend I'm in a movie, like that time at Cape Cornwall when I pretended to be Demelza from Poldark.

-I also know the Fancy rap by Iggy Azaela off by heart. Different strokes for different folks my man.

-I also know the Yeo Valley yoghurt advert rap off by heart and feel quite passionately about it.

-Sometimes I do things badly intentionally so I don't get asked to do them again.

-I think Piano classical BANGS. Ludovico Einaudi is the king.

-I like art galleries and Shakespeare and long walks in the wild. Someone making me laugh, being held but being allowed to be alone. I like it when I don't have to be strong for once.

-I like warm, not hot, rice pudding.

-My relationship with food is always going to be something I have to stay on top of and keep working on. If not mentally then physically.

-Top songs ever: Mirrors-Justin Timberlake, Good Girl- Aquilo, Summer -Calvin Harris, Both Sides Now -Joni Mitchell, Nobody to Love –Sigma.

-Time is just a social construct.

-The collective unconscious theory is one of my favourite concepts of all time.

-I love the romantic British film era that was Love Actually, Notting Hill, Bridget Jones Diary and Four weddings and a funeral. EURGH SO GOOD WHAT A TIME TO BE ALIVE.

Your turn now. (But write it like nobody's watching okay? This is just for you. I'm sharing some of mine for the GREATER GOOD OF THE PEOPLE. Please accept my sacrifice and go start your damn list. Please.)

LESSON 23: ANOTHER YOU IN THE ROOM.

Okay, so you're starting to get to know yourself now. This relationship is progressing pretty nicely. You're learning how to hang out with yourself and go on dates with yourself and make shit fun just for the sake of it.

It's time we step it up a notch bbys.

What's the most important thing in any *healthy* relationship?

A willingness to drop everything to find you a chocolate milkshake from Maccies even when the mAcHinE iS brOkEn at every local store? A devotion to listening to you emotionally explain a TikTok you saw earlier about a cat defending his dog friend from another dog by swiping it in the face until he left him alone? Getting matching tattoos of Spongebob on your buttcheeks?

Okay no, it's trust.

I'd like you to introduce you to yourself, like an imaginary friend almost. I want you to find the absolute best version of you. What do they look like? What are they wearing? What's their body language like, facial expressions? How do they make you feel to be around them?

And most importantly: what would they do or say for you right now that would make you feel better? (Because You Already Know What You Need To Do).

It might be helpful to give them a name, 'mini-me' or 'my higher self' are good ones. Maybe your childhood nickname (BBQ Rebs)? Find what works for you, it's cool, it's only you who is watching. Whatever helps you connect with them.

You're going to bring your mini-me into the picture when you're feeling stressed, overwhelmed, confused, frustrated or even in crisis. I want you to imagine them sitting next to you. What do you need right now? Maybe they give you a hug, or hold your hand, or wrap you up in an invisible blanket? Maybe they put their hands to your heart and encourage you to breathe calmly with them.

What do you need to hear? "You're doing so great right now", "I can imagine this is upsetting for you, I think that's a very natural reaction", "Be gentle with yourself today, you've got a lot going on". Start speaking to yourself like a therapist would. No more judgy comments and sarcastic quips to hide the hatred you feel towards yourself. Just love. Compassion. Forgiveness. Understanding.

What would the best version of you say to someone ELSE going through what you are right now? To a friend or family member, or even a stranger? It wouldn't be "Get over it" or "You're just too sensitive", so why are you treating yourself like that?

Having Another You In The Room is a fun and kind way to get to know yourself better and learn how to treat yourself more kindly.

If physical touch is your love language, visualise them putting a reassuring hand on your shoulder, or crouching down to floor level to talk with you. Sometimes my mini-me just holds my face, or strokes my forehead softly until I fall asleep. Just a squeeze of the arms is often enough to bring me back into a more grounded state.

And take note of what they're wearing...sometimes it's an outfit you were wearing from a memory. Your subconscious clearly thought you were doing a good job then, even if you didn't.

Creating this positive association with yourself is a great start to learning to trust who you are. To learning to trust that you can save yourself, you can ground yourself, you can get yourself out of difficult situations and that you can make safe decisions when you listen to your soul.

You're doing better than you think.

Love, BBQ Rebs.

LESSON 24: STORYTELLING LOVE INTO EXISTENCE

I didn't want to wake up. Henry Cavill had finally showed me, his girlfriend, to the world. It was public. Official. He bought me flowers and an apartment and was completely besotted with me. He held an umbrella over my head when it rained, and wined and dined me where everyone could see. He was so proud of me. He thought I was amazing. And the sex…phwoarrrr. I was completely in love. This was the best dream I had ever had. I didn't want to wake up.

But I did. And the weird thing was – I was still in love. Completely and utterly in love. Not with him, or anyone in particular – just…love. It filled my whole body from head to toe, I smiled non-stop the whole day. I felt so good about myself, I was so proud of myself, I thought I was amazing. I wanted to give all of my joy to others around me. Sparks of light shot out of my fingers with everything I touched. (Was I on drugs?).

I was in love the whole damn day. From the feeling I had cultivated in a dream with Henry Cavill. How on earth was this possible?

I thought love was something we received from someone else. I thought love was a reward for getting things right, behaving the way you're 'supposed to' in a relationship. I thought love was for the lucky ones. I thought love was for 'normal people', not me. I thought love was months of seeking, searching, hunting. Like a mystical creature with rumoured sightings.

I never thought love was inside me the whole time.

But alas, there it was. Loud and proud and shining bright. "HI I'M HERE. I'VE ALWAYS BEEN HERE. Thanks for SEEING me, finally!".

When Henners started to fade from my memory, the feeling remained. I remembered it, and played with it for several days after because of how good it felt. Learning to cultivate that power is a gift you cannot refuse yourself.

You're not all going to be blessed with Henry Cavill's presence in your sleep, but don't worry, I have another plan for those less fortunate, or for when the feeling fades.

I want you to try storytelling love into existence. Not romantic love or a partner, self-love. (It's all the same thing really...we'll get to that later).

Now, the way you make that happen involves a little creativity. A little fantasizing. You can make up a 'fake boyfriend running through the rain and stopping traffic for you' scenario BUT it can't be about them. Their purpose in your fantasy is to remind you of the feeling of love you ALREADY HAVE inside you. Just a little reminder, then off they go.

Those love songs on the radio? They're about you now. I want you to sing them with so much intensity that any passerby would thing you ARE in fact in a very public relationship with Henry Cavill.

"He knelt to the ground and pulled out a ring" - you knelt to the ground and pulled out a ring for you bitch.

"And darling I will be loving you 'til we're 70", yes you will be, loving yourself that is.

"Love your curves and all your edges, all your perfect imperfections" HELL YEAH YOU DO.

You don't need anybody else to love you in order to know love. You don't need another to feel love because they are simply activating the love that we already have within us – WE ARE LOVE. You can be the person that tells you "It's going to be okay" when you need to be rescued from your overwhelm. You can be the person that lovingly makes you a cup of tea in the morning, or rubs your feet before you go to bed.

One of my favourite, silly and eventually utterly hysterical things I do when I'm going to bed alone and getting the wobblies, is saying goodnight to my furniture and imagining they're saying it back.

"GOODNIGHT WARDROBE!" I cry out, smiling awkwardly. "GOODNIGHT TOILET!" I start to giggle. "HOPE YOU SLEEP WELL OVEN!". *Fits ensue*. "YOU DID A GREAT JOB TODAY WINDOW!" *wets self due to hysterical laughter*, you get the picture.

The idea is that everything is love, and love is everything. I need you to get so good at convincing yourself that love is everywhere, that you never question it again. So good at knowing how much love you have for yourself that you'll never settle for anything less than what you deserve in someone else. So good at being in your own company, that it actually feels kinda icky sharing your time with anyone else, so that only *really special* people get that honour.

This isn't just about protecting your energy, this is about cultivating it to benefit you as best as you can. (And if you're still scared of being selfish and/or haven't read part one yet, when YOU are happier, the people around you benefit too).

I fucking love you, fridge.

LESSON 25: INNER POLARITY

I haven't been crazy woo-woo since the start of the book (I had to scare off the ones who weren't meant to be here), but it's time, we're back.

Even if you don't believe in it, I encourage you to read this chapter and remain open minded, you never know, something just might resonate.

The concept of masculine and feminine energy has travelled right through time, from the ancient Mayans to Carl Jung archetypes and beyond. We all have masculine and feminine energy within us, although it isn't necessarily related to men and women, but more the behaviour of each energy itself.

Masculine energy is for *doing*. Getting shit done. Logical rational reasoning, hard and fast. 'Will do anything to get the things I want even if it means taking people out on the way' vibes. It's a high energy, driven and active space. It is disciplined, analytical and on occasion, aggressive. It can be a good space to cultivate joy. Structure and stability is important. Strength and stress are where the masculine thrives.

Feminine energy is for *being*. It is soft and gentle. Decisions are fluid and based on intuition and gut feeling. Empathy and creativity lead this pattern. It can also be passive and sometimes dark and depressive.

Embodiment and connection to everything bigger than the body is important. The feminine wants to roll in the forest or flow with the current of the ocean. Nature and being at one with everything, including challenging emotions, are all part of the feminine.

The intention with polarity is not to be balanced all the time, but to find a way for both parts to work together, collaborate and cooperate through the ebb and flow of life and all it might bring. You might need to be more in your masculine when you are training for a marathon, or more in your feminine when a loved one is passing.

We are all likely to work better with one polarity slightly more dominant than the other based on our personality and lifestyle. The trouble comes when you permanently live a life in only one polarity, or in a polarity that doesn't honour who you really are.

You cannot be an artist if you are so fixated on how much money you will make, the business plan, the studios you are going to sell, what the logical path to making it happen is that you never actually make the art. Art and creativity mean surrendering to your feminine, to trusting and flowing. Whilst there's no harm in logic, creativity is not logical. It is magical and unruly. It has no limits. Masculine energy will not get you there alone.

Likewise, you cannot start a successful book shop if you feel like you have to read a thousand books to find the ones with the right 'energy'. Although that is a commendable dedication to the feminine, putting off the logical, rational side of a business for the sake of years waiting until you (and the books) are ready, will not do anything for your bank account, dream or means of survival.

Incorporate both parts. Connect with both sides. Tune in so finely to yourself that you know where you are at and what you need.

A lack of masculine energy comes across as a lack of direction, drive and discipline. Feelings of hopelessness, low energy and a tendency to 'stay small' and quiet may occur. You may have no big projects in the pipeline, nor feel the energy to pursue any.

A heightened state of masculine energy may lead to controlling, manipulating or domineering behaviour. Acting without thinking, being short-tempered or defensive. Minimal connection with emotions or the self and prioritising a fear of failure over everything is linked to this.

(Of course there are many, many other factors as to why you might be feeling like this, this is merely a theory that may or may not resonate with you, and either way that is fine. Psychology and mental health absolutely take priority when it comes to unhealthy functioning, then we can look to spirituality. Please don't cancel me.)

A lack of feminine energy may present as anxiety, insecurity or jealousy. Lack of self-worth and meaning, poor boundary setting and a fear of abandonment. People pleasing or manipulation from a place of fear, confusion and powerlessness can occur. Creativity is rare or misguided.

A heightened state of feminine energy can mean you get so consumed and lost in creativity that real life is often dismissed. Escapism, living in a fantasy and obsessive daydreaming are all common. You can become overinvolved in your emotions, with a lack of separation between your inner mind and the outer world.

As I mentioned, sometimes there are times where we need an imbalance, but this isn't a healthy way to function full-time. Not being able to connect with your emotions or on the other end of the spectrum, being too over-involved in them, are not comfortable ways to go about life. Finding a way for the polarities to blend together is much more fun and conducive for a happy life.

So how do we 'blend' polarities, or help them collaborate?

The first step is recognising where you are lacking, and where you are more dominant. There is a school of thinking that the right brain (which runs the left side of the body) is where feminine energy dominates. And thus the left brain (running the right side of the body) is dominated by the masculine. In this sense, perhaps you are more prone to aches, pains and injuries on one side of the body to the other? That can often be a good clue.

Acupuncture, Reiki or Craniosacral therapy is another way to understand how the energy channels in your body work, as the whole concept is based on an energy system, and as experienced professionals, they will often be able to pick up a lot more than you can.

Once you are aware of your imbalances, you can then start making active changes to incorporating both polarities into your life. Is a dominant feminine energy making you feel out of control and lost? Start writing lists, planning and budgeting – immediately stepping you straight into your masculine.

Is your dominant masculine energy pushing you far too hard in work and life, leading you to burnout? Slow down, reevaluate the way you spend your time, and schedule more time for you. Choose activities like slow, warm baths. Reading a book in a woodland with a nourishing picnic. Or taking up an art class.

I'm sharing this topic with you because it has really helped me live a better life. It's shown me how to step into my creativity with courage and truth. And also to create a structure for my life that works for me and honours my own traits, needs and goals. It's made it a lot easier to flow and be present with life, whilst knowing that I'm heading in the right direction too.

And when I'm not quite feeling aligned, I have the chance to tune in now and really listen to where I am lacking, and what my body, and soul, needs.

Dating yourself means confronting all the parts of yourself, the good, the bad and the shadow. The process is a blessing in disguise, and will only lead you to a greater truth within yourself if you just keep going.

LESSON 26: GET INTO YOUR BODY

It is very easy to see the physical body, all the bones and organs and blood cells, as separate to your emotional one. It's easy to keep them in two different boxes, with two different diagnoses. It's easy to assume they aren't related to each other and can't communicate together.

And then we see studies linking gut health to happiness[xvii], the link to muscular tension and emotion[xviii], or the way the colours we see can directly affect our perception of a drug's efficacy[xix]. And maybe, because science says so, we start to make a link. We start to feel an enhanced connection between the body, its functions, and how we feel.

But what if it goes deeper than that? Way, way deeper than that? What if it goes so deep that our own minds have the capacity to heal us?

Listen, it's far-fetched, and I certainly haven't accomplished this yet, but I have felt the profound physical benefits of sound-healing, meditation and energy healing. There is some magic here.

Connection to the body itself can allow for a path of healing just as it is. When you first start to communicate with your body, your world will change. When you first start to look inwards and answer questions like "Where in my body feels the safest right now?", or "Where in my body am I feeling tension right now?", it will open a whole new world.

I have had an awful lot of practice with this, and have had some phenomenal teachers, so let me give you a quick demonstration of the kind of awareness you can achieve as the average Joe like me:

Right now in my body my feet are my safe place. There is a strong and grounded energy there that is pulsing and fuelling support through my body. My hips are aching, subtly, but I am aware of it. My womb is working away like a busy bee, I can feel her seeking out the energy in my abdomen and deciding what to do with it. My sacrum feels very calm, there is some healing work happening there and I feel a throbbing connection to my heart as I write that.

My collarbone and shoulders are tired and heavy, they ache with an exhaustion that has carried me through too much, and need a break. They are waiting for me to relinquish some of my over prominent masculine energy and surrender to a world where I don't feel such an intense desire to control. I've made huge shifts there recently.

My heart and throat feel completely at one with each other. Stoic, resilient, stable. My mind feels alive and I am conscious of a slight swelling of my face. My hands still hold a lot of fear, and remain tense and clamped as a result. I know this is a space I need to work with in my healing journey. As one, I feel settled, my nervous system is on guard, but relaxed. I notice the way I feel when I write, and how perfect that feels for me.

Although I wouldn't expect you to be able to pick all of this up within your own body straight away, I hope this shows you the kind of awareness you have the capacity to have. Good ways to begin to connect with this are through mindfulness, self-massage, grounding, sitting with yourself in water or even journalling the subtle changes you notice in your body throughout each day (and finding if they link to anything!).

I want you to develop such a hot sense of awareness about how your body feels that you can notice straight away when your body doesn't feel safe in a situation. "Oo! There's my throat feeling tight, time for me to step away." or "Hmm, I'm clenching my hands, what's triggered that?".

If you are in the position where you are able to respect that your body isn't comfortable and leave, then what a gift and great service you are doing for yourself. If you can't escape, you can tune in to that feeling and try and establish how you can settle it. Is it rational, or is this based on non-repeating past experiences in this place/with this person? Is my body being overprotective right now or is it absolutely on cue with how I feel about this emotionally too? Is my body giving me better cues than my mind has the capacity to right now?

Your body and mind are a team. And the sooner you see that, the easier things will become. What a great service you are doing to yourself to tune in the way you are.

Connecting within in such a way is not only a beautiful way to cultivate self-love, but it's also a great way to know your truth. Is this intuition or is it anxiety? Am I truly respecting and honouring my own boundaries here if my body is screaming no?

Once you have established this connection, you can have a little play with self-healing too. Directing positive energy to pain points and headaches (obviously speak to medical professionals if you have health problems that need addressing), holding your hands over sore spots, aching wombs or tender muscles. Light touch massages are also great for healing, and getting to know ALL of your body – the parts you've never seen or touched before. Finding beauty in it all and a desire to connect with everything.

You could even work with a myofascial trauma release specialist, or a trauma informed yoga teacher to release emotions from the body too. Somatic therapy or craniosacral healing are also great options. And intuitive dance and movement is another great way to physically shift any emotional heaviness.

The journey to mind-body connection is truly an unlimited, beautiful adventure. Don't let taboo and shame and fear stop you from building an even deeper connection to the most important person in your life: you.

SIT WITH IT

PART 5: RELATIONSHIPS

When I tell you I stumbled trying to write this part... Who am I to give relationship advice? Who is anyone? The longer I've been alive, the more I've learnt that not everything is as it seems. The couple that have been together for 30 years and seem like the cream of the relationship crop could both be having affairs behind each other's back. Likewise, the couple that have been together 2 years could be developing a therapeutic healing relationship that will serve them for life.

Relationships don't always end because they've 'failed', but because people have grown into such secure versions of themselves that actually, parting ways is the best thing they could do. And sometimes, 'the one who got away' will in fact be the one who comes back and spends the rest of their life with you.

I believe that going into a relationship with the intention of it being forever is outdated, unhealthy and patriarchal. But at the same time, I also feel that people run away from relationships far too quickly simply because it's begun to uncover core wounds that are too painful for individuals to deal with.

I think butterflies in your belly aren't cute but actually symptoms of anxious attachment and co-dependence, and that healthy relationships should be led by an overwhelming feeling of peace and calm instead. But I also feel like the importance of nurturing, understanding and communicating about your romantic *sex* life should take priority over even day to day conversations.

So, I'll say it again. Who am I to give relationship advice? Who is anyone?

I'm young. But still I could sit here and fill these pages with the failed loves and the broken loves and the messy loves and the dangerous loves. I could fill them with the 'I'll never forget you' loves and the fiery loves and the ones who destroyed me loves and the ones who made me who I am today loves. I could tell you about the times I've taken love to therapy, and ended up rediscovering core wounds that have simply been triggered by my own vulnerabilities. I could tell you about the times I've taken love with me in loneliness, worn it like a handbag and glorified all the ways it would save me.

I could tell you that I looked for love in all the wrong places, and found it there. I could tell you the way love has tricked me, seduced me, abused me, written me off. And how it was everything I ever wanted, until I had it, and it looked nothing like the way I thought it would. I could tell you that it took me three deep loves to truly know love. And deep loss and grief to truly see it.

But it would all come back to one thing: the Big Love? The deep love? The true love? It's within. Somebody else purely gives you space to activate that. And it's fucking cliché, and irritating and *eye-rollingly* annoying. But it's because you know I'm right. And it's because you know it's far harder to harness that inner love than it is to harness it within another.

And it's because sometimes the hyper-independence you have taught yourself to survive makes you feel like loneliness is weak behaviour. It's not, it's normal. Just because you can do love without another doesn't mean you should. Just because you love yourself doesn't mean you can't be lonely, or want a relationship.

This book, and my journey in life and loss, has been all about finding the love within. Once you've begun to harness that, sharing that experience with another can be daunting and overwhelming. You might lose yourself for a bit. You might have to start again. You might find out things about yourself you could have never known without love. You might experience feelings you could have never known existed.

It is by no means an easy feat. I'm hoping you've got the message by now that it's not always meant to be easy here. But I also want you to know that there are beautiful moments that haven't happened yet. Incredible people you haven't yet met. Memories that might change your life forever. And love that will open your whole damn heart that you can't even imagine right now.

I'd like to share with you a piece I wrote when I began to know I was ready for love again. I'd been practicing intentional celibacy and intentionally not dating for almost a year. That process allowed me to be ready for what I was calling in. And boy did I call it in.

"It's the days when my breasts are throbbing and my body is shaking with a concoction of unbalanced hormones pulsing through my blood. And I'm cold even when I've pumped the heating up full. It's sitting on the sofa, peering over to the spot where someone else used to sit, where someone else used to welcome me in. At least at the beginning anyway. It's wanting to lie on them. It's wanting them to caress my hair, stroke my forehead and trace my lips with their fingers. Wanting for nothing, just embracing the connection almost subconsciously. It's having someone you feel safe to be weak around. Someone you can let your guard down to. You can relax your shoulders, and all the tense energy you've been holding there from constantly protecting yourself just…falls away. The energy is shed like the lining of your womb. Releasing. Freeing. Calming.

It's wanting to feel for just one moment, that you can let your guard down. You can just relax for five minutes, and let someone else carry your worries for you. Someone to share the burden of life with. As well as the joys of it. The moments where the sun catches their face, in an inconspicuous place, making even the darkest places bright. You could be anywhere. But with them, it's everywhere. You feel invincible. You feel whole. Like nothing can harm you when you have the energy of a pair in love.

I'm imaging him now, massaging my aching back. Carrying me up to bed even when I didn't ask. He just knew. He would make me a herbal tea, he would just know the one I wanted. Spearmint, for hormones. Camomile, for relaxation. He remembered. He paid attention to everything I did without me even realising. I would be his whole world, yet we could still retain our independence. We could be on our own unique journeys through life and be proud of each other. We would never want to hold one another back from our truest potential.

There would be space, when we needed it. Ungoverned, unforced. We would feel safe enough to walk away and give each other time to process our inner workings. There would be a beauty in watching each other's internal journeys. A pride in seeing the people we were becoming.

He's reading his book in bed. Something he's passionate about. I've drunk my herbal tea now and I'm just lying on his chest. Tracing his skin, the way it ebbs and flows. He allows my discomfort. He acknowledges my pain. Every now and then, he lowers his book and kisses me lightly on the forehead. Watching me think. He admires my strength, as I admire his courage.

It is the only place I have ever felt safe. It is the only place I have let my guard down. I have let myself be sad. It doesn't take away from my power, it doesn't destroy my internal being. It lets the light in. Through my wounds and through my pain and through my tears. And as I cry, he holds me tighter. He puts his book away, puts his head on the pillow beside mine and just stares into my eyes. Reassuring me with his gaze. Promising this isn't permanent. There is an admiration in his watch at the powerful feminine energy I am allowing myself to feel after all these years of being too strong. All this time. He knows how much this means to me. He knows how much growth I am experiencing and how much it has taken me to get to this point.

I am exposed. But I am whole. And I can breathe.

And this would be us."

Six months later, I wrote a follow up piece.

"We talked about astrology a lot. Something I had been studying for a few months to get a qualification, something he had been passionate about for years before we'd even met. And I had no idea. We talked about what I needed from someone's chart, carefully making sure it wasn't the same as his. That wasn't what this was. We weren't dating. We were friends that fucked. Best friends it seemed. Over a weekend.

When he left, once again, I felt calm. I felt like my soul had just got out of a deep, relaxing, magnesium infused bath. And every part of me had been refuelled. My dog, who had been suffering with on and off anxiety prior to now, was like a different animal. I actually thought she was unwell for a moment.

I didn't need to see him again. I accepted how temporary everything was. I didn't message him, didn't need to. He made me calm.

But also, he made me talk.

He made me cut open my fucking heart and get damn honest with myself. About the truths and the lies and the deceptiveness and the resentment and the bitterness that I was hiding that was holding me back. He was the king of Shadow-work.

Healing happens in safety. Healing happens in calm, understanding connections such as ours.

That could've been the last time I ever saw him, and it would be fine. I felt so grateful and honoured for the things he had awakened in me in that short period of time that I didn't need anything more.

The respect I had. The parts of ourselves that we never knew were desperate to meet each other, share those conversations, without feelings or ulterior motives… They had been blessed. And I will be forever grateful for that. Simply knowing him was enough.

But it wasn't to be the last time we met. Not even close in fact. One month in and we were exclusive. It felt easier together. It made more sense together. But it was also fine apart. It was so surreal.

We went on so many walks, we got lost together. We took long drives late at night to see the stars and spent hours in passionate debates about the meaning of life. We got coffee and cooked together and I began to find him hilarious as we became more and more relaxed around each other. I stopped being scared. I stopped holding back. He cracked me open and my heart flowed out of every cell in my body. Like a bright light that had been in darkness for years. It was piercing and powerful and warm, so warm.

I would come downstairs after a shower, and he would be lying on my sofa, etched out six-pack lined by sunlight piercing through the blinds on a Saturday morning, reading a National Trust book. It was like I had always known. That he would be there. My match. My mirror.

I was finding the love within me that I'd been cultivating inside

for years.

And trusting someone with it. For the first time in my life."

It doesn't matter if it's not forever. It really doesn't. What matters is that you were brave enough to let it in and let it change you. You were brave enough to bare your soul and your truth and your brokenness and even the parts of you that you don't know how to love yet.

To feel love is the greatest gift human experience can give you. Be it in loss, or in life. Let it move you, and see what happens.

LESSON 27: THE SCIENCE OF LOVE

I'm an emotional thinker. More often than not, I look within for the answers rather than to what 'everyone else says'. But some topics curate so much inner complexity and confusion that I NEED to know what everyone else says, and by that, I mean the science. And by 'some topics', I mean love.

The big challenge with love, particularly early-stage love, is that we are not being led from within so much, but from chemicals. From hormones. From 'the right DNA match', not the right soul match. It's part of why it's so easy to get it wrong. The 'right DNA match' can even be dependent on what medications you're taking. The contraceptive pill for example can skew your senses, making you choose a partner who doesn't quite fit as well as the original biological plan intended[xx].

According to science[xxi], we are drawn to partners who are genetically dissimilar to us and who have compatible immune systems to ours. It's a viable offspring thing. Our bodies want us to choose a partner who is most likely to produce (or help to produce) healthy children. Thus, once the initial spark has been lit, it is hormones and chemicals that drive us together initially. This is what we know more commonly as: The Honeymoon Phase. Love starts in the brain, not the heart.

The honeymoon phase can last from six months to several years to not even happening at all. It is designed to pump you with just the right amount of hormones through lust, passion and attraction for you to actually get the time and interaction to *attach* to one another. You know, to actually like each other as people, not just because someone is giving you attention or a good boning.

It is that blurry dopamine fuelled beginning that can be a little dangerous for the psyche. Known to have similar addiction responses to Class A drugs[xxii], the honeymoon phase can have you forgetting who you are, quite literally. The fixation on the reward (the partner), combined with insecure attachment types can create co-dependency, emotionally or physically abusive relationships, adultery and more, as the areas of the brain involved with critical thinking, self-awareness and rational behaviour get turned off[xxiii].

Obviously, there's a lot more to it than simply science. And there's a lot more science out there on this topic than I can fit in this chapter, or can properly break down and understand as the non-scientist that I am. Personality types, past traumas, cultural and social implications, your upbringing, your moral values - they all have a part to play in relationship success. But I think most of us who have been on the relationship Ferris wheel will recognise the feeling you get when two or three years in, you realise you never really knew your lover in the first place. And for that, you can blame science, mostly.

Let's say you get through the early dating phase, arguably one of the most challenging times to stay grounded and true to yourself (and maybe you aren't supposed to). According to one theory[xxiv], after early dating comes 'The Settling Phase' as the hormones and pretences cool off. Then 'Committing and Building', where you create a life structure together, kids, houses, marriage, travel etc. etc. Perhaps the most significant stage next: 'Breaking Out', reconnecting back to who you really are and recognising the ways you have held yourself back because of the relationship. And finally, as a result, 'Repairing or Leaving', which is self-explanatory really.

Just because you can get through these phases doesn't necessarily mean you are doing it in a healthy way without over sacrificing yourself or over compromising. But it's a helpful way to visualise the structure of one way that intimate relationships can unfold at least.

Am I telling you to completely disregard the first six to eighteen months of a relationship because of how completely and utterly blind it can make you? No. Am I suggesting that you be more conscious about how grounded and rational you are during that period and probably walk with caution when making big decisions together? Maybe.

Social connections are so important to humans. Which is super annoying to some of us introverts with trust issues. But because of how innately driven we are to connect, we can end up surrendering ourselves and self-abandoning who we are purely because we want to be around someone else. Someone who will pay us attention. Somone who will validate us and make us feel good. Someone who will share our interests and conversations and friendships and memories. Someone who will sexually satisfy us, cook and provide for us, help raise our children (or maybe just do it for us).

Apart from showing patience, nothing about the above statements that made you feel all warm and fuzzy are anything about your partner themselves. About who *they* are, what their values are, the things they bring to the world, the way they navigate conflict and harmony or whether they are nice to waiters and servers.

What about their CORE beliefs? What about their CORE wounds? What about *their* 'Getting to know myself' list? What about their shadow-work and their big mistakes and their book of lessons learnt?

I'm being a bitch to you right now because I too have sat myself in relationships before that were entirely based off my own insecurities. I thought I knew them, that was enough. But really, I was holding on tight as hell because I loved that attention. I needed it. I didn't actually know how to survive without it. Luckily, if you're in this boat, it's highly likely you're not the only one in it feeling this way. And there is fabulous self-discovery journey up ahead.

Take the science. Take all the pieces we have put together so far in this book and sit with it. Is there a way you can love without the addiction? Without the false leads and fake connections? Is there a 'why' in your relationship bigger than 'they give me an emotional high?'

And if you're not sure, there's a fun game in my house where someone says 'I love you' in a cutesie romantic moment under the stars with the crickets chirping, and the other, without taking a breath, will shoot out: "WHY?".

LESSON 28: I DON'T WANT TO BE YOUR EVERYTHING

I don't want to be put on a pedestal. I don't want to be everything you've ever wanted.

I want to love sober. I want to love messy. I want you to see my damage, my pain, my past. Without it being clouded by the drug addiction-esque ride that is 'the beginning'.

Make knowing me the beginning. Don't leave it until the rush fades, and we're left to look around at the dull greys we painted with dopamine, figuring out how we're going to navigate them.

Teach me to slow down. Teach me to feel safety in being incomplete. See all of my human. Whilst knowing that I will never be yours to keep. I'm not to be owned or guaranteed, none of us are.

So see me as right now. Not as my potential. Not as who I am without my past. Not as binding to each other to hide our pain and then confusing that as love. And in this slow, messy, sometimes painful journey to getting to know one another as we are, let us love our truth.

*

Pedestals come from fear. Pedestals come from a sense of

unworthiness. Is love worth it if you don't feel worth it? What if it isn't about the rush and the high and the chase and the longing. What if it's just meant to be peaceful?

When I called in love, I wanted someone who would lead an army with me. Not in front of me, not behind me, but with me. It's complicated, because we have different roles to play, but just because our roles are different doesn't make them any less worthy than the other. Getting yourself and someone else to be fully on board with that concept can be a challenge. But not impossible, and maybe, just maybe, worth waiting for.

I don't believe in 'You're my everything's and 'I couldn't live without you's. You can live without them, you already have, and you will again if you need to. It won't be the end of the world, just the end of a chapter, and maybe a difficult one. Like other difficult chapters you have already been through, and will go through again.

I believe that people remain in your life for as long as you need to learn from them, and they you. Maybe that is 'forever', but maybe it isn't. And maybe that's okay, normal in fact. Maybe we do put far too much pressure on relationships and in fact, we are supposed to have multiple deep and intimate experiences with other humans in our lifetime.

Pedestals can make your boundaries weak. They are your 'everything' so it's fine, right? They can get away with x,y and z? Pedestals can make you focus more on how they make you feel, rather than who they actually are (and listen, feeling good around them is a green flag, but also could be dependent on so much more than their interaction with you – you cannot use feeling as a sole indicator that a relationship is healthy or right).

If you really can't live without them what does that make you? A conjoined twin? A baby roo to a kangaroo? In the early stages of a relationship, grounding will be hard and blurry and kind of a grey area, which is why it is so important to experience the Breaking Out phase. The 'reminding myself that I am my own badass individual who can do a lot of tough stuff with or without a man' phase.

Pedestals create anxiety. Pedestals leak a fear of leaving, or death or cheating or some other random and terrifying reason why you may not be together forever.

You may not be together forever. I don't care how good you are, how solid you are, how sure you are, how healthy you are, how safe and careful you are. You may not be together forever. And it will by no means be easy if that does happen. But it won't be impossible, because you have you. This whole time you have you. You've had you the whole time. You'll have you right up until the end and beyond.

And do you know what you can do to support yourself when the line between your own self-identity and making the relationship your identity gets blurred? You can practice grounding yourself. You can become so consumed in the present that nothing scares you anymore. You can surround yourself with gratitude for the right now and memory making for the right now.

You can date yourself WITHIN a relationship. You can make special alone time for you and keep THAT relationship healthy too.

Rather than putting someone on a pedestal because you're trapped in the fantasy of their potential, start a relationship by finding all the reasons you aren't right for each other. All the things you aren't a fan of in the way they work. Write a list if you need to (and include your own flaws too and whether they would be compatible with future Partner Pedestal).

Recognise as many flaws as you can from what you know of them now - we can't predict them all, we all have hidden sides that only come out under intense stress, change or transformation. And then ask yourself, honestly and with all the strength you have, if you *could* be in a relationship where those flaws are always there. They never change, they never go away, they are always there.

Can you really cope with the lack of communication when you are a big communicator?

Can you really stand the lack of commitment when you are looking to settle down?

Can you work with their trauma, and all the unpredictable times that may resurface? Do you have capacity for that at this time in your life?

What if they are always a messy person? And no matter how many times you ask them to change, they never ever will. Do their positives outweigh their negatives enough for you to be able to tolerate those flaws?

You have to go into a relationship with the attitude that they may never change. Because dating someone for their potential is dangerous, and harmful to both parties. That person might be perfectly happy with the way they run their life, then all of a sudden, BOOM, it's criticism central and they begin questioning their own self-worth.

People have bad habits, that's a fact. But it's not your job to change them, nor is it your job to tolerate them if it doesn't sit well with you. Expecting someone to change in order to fit your ideal fantasy relationship is like playing with Barbies. Not people.

No relationship will be without its issues, its core wounds, that's unrealistic. But you are strong enough to decide what kind of issues you are willing to work with, and the ones you aren't.

And as much as it is extremely challenging choosing to walk away from someone who makes your heart sing, sometimes you have to let your head have a say in relationships as well.

And if you really, really, want a pedestal, at least make sure you're on it too.

LESSON 29: SELF-ABANDONMENT AND BREAKING OUT

Sometimes, when something makes you feel so good that you're scared you're going to lose it, you can lose yourself instead. It's a bitter sacrifice, but it happens.

Many of us don't feel worthy of love, which in my eyes is one of the greatest tragedies of humanity. Love is the most magical thing we have, yet self-hatred often stops us from truly knowing it.

The peculiar behaviour of self-abandonment means we often don't recognise we're even doing it until we're not. Others may notice and even pull us up on it, but we feel good, we feel safe, so how can what we're doing be wrong in any sense?

Our worst habits were once our best attempts to make ourselves feel safe. Self-abandonment is no exception.

For those of us with core wounds along the lines of unworthiness and rejection, having someone 'pick you' can feel like a fantasy, not real, like you are dreaming. And when life has felt like a nightmare, of COURSE it's natural to want to stay in that dream for as long as you can.

Sometimes life can have been so exhausting, so traumatising (whether on the outside or on the inside – the mind is a powerful thing) that you will sacrifice everything to keep on this side of survival. You'll sacrifice friends, family, hobbies, habits, beliefs, even your physical wellbeing. Because the one single thing that is dominating your energy is doing everything you can to stay in a relationship.

We are wired to survive. Some of us have been living believing the world is on fire because our minds have been trapped in that way of seeing the world, potentially after years of it being a reality as children. So we keep running and running, desperately hoping to get away from the fire, taking everything out in our way in order to just keep going.

It's real hard to get our bodies to learn that there is no fire anymore. It's real hard to stop running.

You won't find a home outside of yourself until you find one within. No place, no person, no job, no hobby, no experience. You have to start by making yourself feel safe. Only then can you truly know yourself. And knowing how to belong to yourself might just be the most important thing in the world.

Self-abandonment within relationships can look like many things, but most commonly looks like abandoning our own self-love practices and rituals in favour of retaining someone else's attention.

There is an element of self-abandonment that comes with having children of course, but generally the motives there are fuelled less around your own survival, but of your children's, which is fair enough.

Sometimes I wonder if a smidge of self-abandonment within a new relationship (or at least in your first relationships) is necessary. Because it leads to the most wonderful Breaking Out experience that can be quite transformative.

Breaking Out is the moment you realise you haven't danced with yourself in months. That the book you were loving has been sat untouched on the bedside table since you met. That you stopped going to Sunday morning Yoga because you wanted to spend time with them.

Breaking Out is realising you haven't asked yourself 'How are you?' in far too long. It is returning your heart to your journal after months of brief sentences to summarise your day because your soul was elsewhere. It's realising the dreams you have aren't aligned with the life you've ended up living and wondering how you got there.

It is the individuation process of a couple that will quite literally make or break them. And I dig it. It roars with the sound of courage and authenticity and all of a sudden remembering yourself. It's admitting you'd got a bit lost and choosing to recalibrate.

Self-abandonment can truly be the initiation process of love. Because when you wake up in that good ol' Breaking Out phase, you might find that you never truly loved that person in the first place, that it was just the hormones and the science and really, you can't stand how messy they are and it hurts your soul to have to put up with it.

Or, you wake up (and it's completely out of the blue and unravels over several weeks as the amnesia wears off by the way) and you realise how much your behaviour is inhibiting them. How much your control and micro-management and power games to keep everything in your favour have actually just been hammering against all the things you love about that person. And as much as it's confusing and alarming, it's also a refreshing reset on your love, and is just the BEGINNING of a deep and intimate connection.

When the chemicals of love wear off, or the fear of abandonment subsides as you begin to find a home within yourself, everything will look very different. But everything will also be far more real.

At first it might just be an inside voice, a small and niggling conversation. It might just be picking up your paintbrush for the first time in 18 months, holding your chest as you remember the nostalgic way the brush strokes make your heart sing. Whatever it is, it will find you if you let it. You will always find your way back to yourself.

And perhaps that small conversation within turns to booking yourself onto a pottery class, alone, even on 'couple time'. Perhaps it's asking them to walk the dog you both own so that you can take up Belly Dance, make friends for you, or simply go and read a book in a field somewhere and remember what it's like to be alone with yourself.

Perhaps self-abandonment was simply a pause in the journey to getting to know yourself, and now you've pressed play again, you just get to meet yourself all over again. You can ask what it was like to fall in love like that – how you felt, how you ached, how you yearned. You can gossip with your heart like teenage girls after a first date. You can come back to yourself, whenever you are ready to.

The consequences of breaking out can be varied. Either; your partner will not be the person you remembered them to be (remember, you were under the influence of hormones when you met, forgive yourself), you will not be the person your partner remembers you to be (subservient, overly-forgiving, a pushover), or you will both fall in love all over again.

Observe carefully the look – no, the feeling, your partner experiences when they first see you doing something for you. Although you may be greeted by surprise or shock initially, watching you honour your truth is super-sexy. And it allows and encourages them to honour theirs too. (If your partner has consistent negative reactions to your self-renewal-experience, conversations may need to be had).

You get to learn even more about each other. You get to find new quirks, old hobbies, forgotten favourites. It has the potential of being a beautiful revelation. One that no doubt will take you a little by surprise at first, but gift you both with greatness, truth and an unwavering honesty in what it is to be your own person.

I congratulate and honour anyone who dives into the brutal divine that is this process.

See you on the other side.

LESSON 30: RISING IN LOVE

It's not butterflies, it's anxiety. And that's a hard pill to swallow. It's not falling in love, it's losing yourself. It's not 'finding the one' but a chemical reaction.

And you know what the craziest thing is? That none of the above mean it won't work. You can have a very viable, healthy relationship AND have the mildly traumatic, head-spinning out of control experience that is The Beginning.

But you don't have to. You can have it all without being obsessed with them. You can have it all without having those moments where you 'wish it could be like it was at the start'. You can have it all without the facetimes 'til 3am, or the 24/7 stalking of their socials.

You can have it all by Rising in Love. With grace, dignity and your feet on the ground. If that's what you want – some people dig the rush and that's cool too. Some of us get triggered by it and find the hyperarousal phase exhausting. So I'm here for all of ya.

'Please, tell us! What is the magic cure to this terrible malady!' (Cue Orsino's Monologue, Act 1, Scene 1 for my fellow Shakespeare addicts).

Well, here's a helpful list I've put together on The Beginning – dating, flirting, courting, whatever you'd like to call it. But that will be useful in many ways to well-established relationships too.

1. Focus less on whether they like you (in fact, not at all if you can), and more or whether YOU LIKE THEM.

This sounds like such a simple trick, but the number of times I'd find myself changing outfits before a first date because I was worried they would think I was 'too slutty', or too 'teachery' or 'too nice' is disturbing. And this is not a unique behaviour. Y'all have done it too. (I just know these things). Forget re-typing messages six times, or searching their Instagram to find their favourite things and conversations to avoid. If they don't like you, as you, then it was never meant to be, and we move on.

2. If you're anxious, you're not ready yet.

This is cruel, sorry, but if you want to beat science at its own game, this is the only way. And listen, you can be a little bit uncomfortable. The same level you would be if you're going to a new place that you don't know very well. But the sweating? The palpitations? The hyperventilating? It's a hard pass. It's a hard, go home, reset your nervous system and try again another time. You gotta meet in safety, with safety.

3. Have a take it or leave it approach.

I want you to be so cool about your life and singlehood, that you really could just take it or leave it when it comes to love. You enjoy spending time with yourself so much that you'd be more than happy if things continued that way. If someone else is going to be part of that, your mind and body have to be on board, and that person has to be pretty special.

4. Get out there

Expose yourself to potential romantic investments on the regular to normalise the feeling in your body. (Of course do this safely, coffee shops are a great low key, short time frame, easy to leave if it's a waste of time dating option). Normalise flirting. Normalise bold questions. Normalise being confident enough to enjoy the game. Doing this will likely reduce the chances of fantasising over 'the one' you've been talking to on Tinder for three weeks with no meet up.

5. Grounding and self-boundaries.

If you begin to feel like you're losing yourself, get grounding your body. Meditation, barefoot walks. Movement. Dance. Writing. Singing. Being with nature or in water. Deep belly breathing. Set self-boundaries; I'll only see him on weekends for now or no visits to my house yet. You could even set communication boundaries: "I won't be checking my phone between 9pm and 9am".

6. Contact when you want to, not when you should.

An absolute winner and game changer for me was not monitoring the way I texted. 'I must reply within an hour but no less than 5 minutes from when he texts me' *rolls eyes*. Text when you want to. When you feel good. When you want to communicate and it feels healthy to. Send x's and o's if you want. Or don't. Honour how you want to communicate. Whether that's straight away now and six hours apart tomorrow because you're busy and don't have the emotional energy. No games. Just truth.

7. Respect your energy

Planned a weekend together but absolutely don't have the energy but terrified they will leave you if you cancel? CANCEL. With honest communication of course, we don't do ghosting here. If they are right for you, and you communicate well, they will understand. Need some mid-week 'you time'? Let them know you need some space and that it isn't personal but that you need to respect your energy. Feel grounded enough for them to stay over another night? Respect that and communicate it.

8. Remember to be girlfriend, not mum or therapist.

Would girlfriend tolerate this? Or is this something mum puts up with? Would girlfriend respond this way? Or is this how a therapist would handle a situation? You are not their mother or their therapist, and no matter how tempting it is to micro-manage their lives (because you know it will function better), it is not your life to manage. And as much as it is tempting to be over-tolerant when they are hurting and constantly exhaust your energy giving that support because they've been through trauma, that is not your role here. What would girlfriend do?

It absolutely is possible to rise in love rather than fall. As long as you keep in touch with your body and your heart, you honour your truth and respect your energy and needs, it can totally be an option for you.

It is normal and healthy to want to be in a romantic partnership. We're only human. But want and need are different things, and it's important to keep reminding yourself of that and checking in with where you're at.

Keep remembering how much love you already have within you, and that you will always be enough, just as you are.

What is for you won't go past you

LESSON 31: BASIC HUMAN NEEDS

There comes a rare event within a relationship where both parties experience big trauma at the same time. For example, one partner has a parent slowly fading with dementia, and the other spouse has been diagnosed with a life changing health condition. In an ideal world, our partner would be there to love and support us through a really challenging experience. In reality, this is truly and utterly the battlefield for relationships. Many don't make it out alive.

What do you do when you've gotten used to a support system always being there, that then vanishes in one of your toughest challenges? How are you supposed to navigate that situation with calmness and compassion, both to yourself, and to your partner? How can you possibly remain sane when it feels like your partner is so consumed in their trauma that they aren't even acknowledging yours?

Well, here's the thing. You don't and you can't. This part of relationships is where shit really hits the fan. Where the passion vanishes and the sex stops and all you can see is a stranger that you happen to be living with who is being super unsympathetic to what you're going through.

Maybe you tried being the patient one. Maybe you've given the compassion and the grace, even though you didn't really have a cup to pour out of. But instead of gratitude, you were rewarded with snappy remarks and sharp tones, a sink full of dirty dishes and a WhatsApp group devoted to how unsupportive you are being.

Maybe you're the snappy one, lashing out in frustration at the complete and utter lack of understanding your partner is giving you. Maybe you're not grieving the way they say you should, and maybe you're sick and tired of hearing it, so spend your evenings watching the Fast and Furious movies back-to-back in complete silence rather than talking to them.

The double-dose trauma treatment is like a lethal injection to love. Because sometimes trauma will bring out a side to someone that really isn't going to work for you, like aggression or infidelity for example. Other times it's the neediness that'll drown you. It's the constant crying out for reassurance and connection that you just don't have the energy to provide.

There is one grounding factor that has helped me make a little more sense of these situations. And it's based on the (slightly outdated but still relevant) Maslow's Hierarchy of Needs. And this is for those moments when you desperately need that support from your partner, or just some basic acknowledgement that you are in fact in a relationship, and you're not getting any of it.

I want you to ask yourself if they are tending to their basic human needs. Are they eating right? Are they getting decent sleep? Are they making sure they've washed their clothes to wear, or cleaned the dishes to use so they are even able to eat? Is their breathing calm and steady? Are they feeling sheltered and safe (including: is their body safe to be in right now, functioning as it should be to give them the best chance at survival?). Are they getting enough rest and downtime (has their mind had some sleep?) Are they keeping up their usual gym and fitness routine, taking care of their body?

If any of these things are unfilled, you cannot expect them to prioritise you and your needs over them. Full stop. They just do not have capacity. And this also applies to you.

If you can keep reminding yourself of this concept when the bitterness and rage creeps in, if you can continue to recognise that they are in survival mode, just like you, then it will ease the resent a little. Sometimes only temporarily. But if you can keep finding that, then you're in a good position. The last thing you need on top of everything you're already dealing with is to be angry at the person you love. It really won't help.

At this point, the only way through is to outsource. You'll have to start thinking about how you managed during crisis when you were single. Who did you reach out to then? Was it a great helpline, or a family member who is great at providing advice or support? Did you go on long walks by yourself, or use your headphones more in the house to have your own private dance parties whilst doing the washing up?

For me, I drive up to a hilltop in the countryside and scream in the car like they do in the movies. No one can hear me, and it feels good. Wild and primal. I like that. I take barefoot walks and grab the earth with my hands until I feel like I am simply part of nature again.

These phases are not supposed to be easy, especially in relationships. You might have to give more than you get for a little while. You might have to take on more responsibilities if you're the one who has more energy available. Or, you might have to sit with the guilt of watching your partner be the one who gives more, whilst knowing there is nothing in you that is able to help right now.

Being able to do this without letting resent take over is not easy. And by no means is this a long-term solution. Sometimes crisis can go on for a year. You cannot be giving more than you get for a year. There has to be moments of respite. Of relief. Of understanding. Of deep and meaningful communication and tough conversations. There has to be room for mistakes and failure and learning without it meaning the relationship has to end.

And listen, I will be the last person to tell you to stay in a relationship longer than you should, but at the same time, we cannot expect relationships to be without hardship. The fairytales and the modern love stories never show the bits where it gets super hard because you're both going through shit you don't know how to deal with individually, let alone as a couple. They never show the tear-soaked conversations in the early hours of the morning, five years into the relationship when you question if you're going to make it through together.

They also don't show the unity and strength that is built on the other side of the hardship. When the commitment you've shown to one another at your worst means more than any ring, any ceremony. You start to walk together with this deep level of understanding. A recognition of hardship only the two of you will truly understand. (And again, that alone is not enough to keep you together, a healthy, loving relationship composes of many things).

In your darkest seasons you might be the live in carer (but know when enough is enough). You will question if this is a storm you can weather. To love is to stay when every cell says "run"! Blinkers on. Facing forward. Wading through. Together.

So here's the low down on the double trauma smackdown: there's literally no right way through, but you must summon all the strength you've got if you want to make it. Remind yourself that you don't truly know how your person is feeling (even if you think you do, and think they should be dealing with it differently – I am certainly guilty of this). Remind yourself that your person is trying their best, just as you are, and that it might look different to how you expect. And remind yourself that you have done hard shit before on your own, without them, without anyone.

And that you know, deep down, you're going to survive it, even if things turn out differently to how you expected. You will still be okay. You will.

LESSON 32: THE LITTLE AFFIRMATIONS OF LOVE LIST

You may be familiar with the concept of love languages[xxv], of which there are five. Words of affirmation, physical touch, acts of service, receiving gifts and quality time. You may be lucky (and observant) enough to have experienced all of these languages in action across your lifetime, through friends, family, and of course romantic relationships.

That friend you have that is always buying gifts for everyone for example, because it's her way of saying she cares about you. Or the boss who books experience days out as bonding activities and as a reward for your efforts rather than bonuses, because that's how they best know how to love.

I would rather take a handwritten intimate birthday card than one with £20 and a signature in it for example (I'm also writing a book to help you...any clues what my primary love language is?).

Love languages are a fabulous concept that massively help understand communication blockages within relationships.

"It's like you're trying to pay a British Newsagents with Euros, but they only accept Pounds" is a way I like to explain the frustration that can occur when different love languages exist within a relationship. "The thought is there, but they won't even register it without an onsite currency exchange."

Different love languages within a relationship can look like:

-Buying flowers for her every week when her love language is physical touch, and wondering why she says 'you don't care about me, you're just trying to buy my love'.

-Cooking them dinner and washing their clothes, expecting them to recognise how much you care, when their love language is words of affirmation.

-Taking time off work to spend time with him, assuming he will see how much you care about him for doing that, but his love language is receiving gifts, and he only gets them on Birthdays and Christmas.

We cannot expect one another to completely change our love languages because of the way we process love. Instead, we have to find a way we can both benefit, and that requires a little bit of learning and a little bit of mindful awareness.

First of all, having the conversation and discerning each other's love languages is key. Sometimes it may take a while for you to figure out what your love language is, but keep a careful eye on where you put your energy into showing your partner love, and it will reveal itself with time. Often we have multiple love languages, rather than just one, but the primary language is generally the one that is most important to you.

Then you have to create your own little currency exchange. (Time to open the notes app again). I call this the Little Affirmations of Love List.

I hear the haters shouting from the side lines; "IF THEY LOVED YOU, YOU'D KNOW" and "THIS IS BARE MINIMUM BEHAVIOUR". But that concept, as well meaning as it is, disregards different love languages, communication styles, neurodivergent minds and more. It's just not as simple as that, and sometimes, as shocking as it is, relationships do require a little bit of work.

It's important to note here that you cannot keep your currency exchange open all the time. That would be exhausting when you are so used to using your own currency. No, your currency exchange is there for the wee moments you feel a little insecure, and need a little reassurance, and your partner is speaking in Euros.

The list is not there as a substitute for (relatively) consistent healthy relationship behaviour, it is just there as a pick me up, and as a reminder for my spiralling anxious babes that they aren't loving you any less because you forgot to pick up the milk, they just communicate their reassurance through a hug rather than words. Because that's the language they speak. And you can't, and shouldn't, change that.

You can structure your list however you'd like, in whatever way is more beneficial to you. You could have a column for all the ways they've shown you love through their love language (which will likely be quite a challenge for you to pick up on if it isn't your natural tongue), or you could have a column for the ways they've shown you love through your love language once you've had that discussion with them – because that's a pretty big deal. If someone is willing to try and learn a new language for you, that's an addition to the list as it is.

Here's some examples of what your list might look like:

-He spontaneously bought me a pomegranate because he knows how much I love them.

-They got me some chickie nuggies on the way home (with BBQ sauce).

-He drove all the way to that garden centre to get me the plant I liked.

-She stopped in at my grandparents to check in on them to save me having to.

-She picked up my suit from the drycleaners for me when I was super busy.

-They said "this is the best birthday I've ever had".

-They said "I'm sorry if I'm being miserable, this week has been tough on me, thanks for being so patient".

-He said "We're lucky to have each other" and put his arms around me.

-He held hands with me in public for the first time.

-She lay on my lap when we watched a movie and it meant so much to me.

-They spent their lunch break with me because I was having a bad day.

-We had a phone free day at the theme park and spent some quality time together.

-She got a babysitter for the kids so we could have a date night as just us.

I hope that your currency exchange blossoms and grows, that you are both able to learn little bits of new languages to help make your relationship sing, and that someone, someday, buys you chickie nuggies.

33: WHAT'S YOUR ROLE?

This one's gonna be controversial. Every person who you have a close relationship with (immediate family, children, partner etc) has an expectation of your role in that relationship. It may not be fair, it may not be right, it may not be healthy, but it exists. It's often never communicated, despite being a major cause of conflict, resent and bitterness.

The role they expect you to play may be insulting and as far from the role you want to play as possible. Or it may be a wakeup call, an 'ah-hah' moment, a cure for all ills.

Let's unravel this.

In Western culture, it is expected that *parents* support, provide for, keep safe, nourish and raise their children. That's a given. That is their role. I think we can all agree on that. When this role gets skewed – for example when a child has to act on behalf of their parent due to alcoholism for example, it can lead to long lasting trauma[xxvi], mental health challenges, behavioural issues and relationship difficulties.

Now, I'm not saying that other incomplete role parts have the same traumatic effect, I'm just highlighting the importance of this one.

Let's take siblings next. As the oldest sibling, there is a different level of responsibility than there is for a younger sibling. It's not quite as extreme as 'keep safe and protect' in the same element as there is for a parent, but there are traces of it. It's more 'wait, let me check first'.

That is their role. There is a reason oldest children are more likely to be leaders[xxvii].

Let's imagine that this role continues into adulthood. This expectation to be there, to support, to look out for. Is it fair? No, but is life?

You're frustrated because your younger sibling never checks up on you. She never texts or calls, it's always you. You feel neglected and left out. Or, on the other side of the frame, she hounds you all the time. She's always asking for help and sometimes it gets too much to handle.

She's asking you to play *your role*, because that's what feels safe for her. It's what you're 'supposed' to be to her. Of course she's not going to text you first – you're her big sibling, you're the one who's supposed to look out for her. Or of course she's going to ask too much of you, because she sees you as a partial caregiver, someone to trust when she is feeling out of control.

I hear you right now – this isn't fair, it's messy and irrational and doesn't factor in our own individual lives and everything we've got going on in them and the support we might be needing at the time...

Exactly. It is messy and it is unfair but that expectation is there whether you like it or not. Ask her. I dare you. Ask her what role she expects you to play in your relationship. What she needs from you.

Only then, when you know where you stand (because every single set of circumstances will be different in each relationship dependent on a gazillion factors) can you set your ground rules. Only then can you create compromise and make adjustments.

You can, calmly and with compassion, reinvent your relationship contract to make sure both parties are playing their parts, in the best way that looks for you both. I'll be honest with you, this could take years to get right. You may not even get an answer when you ask. You may get 'I don't need you for anything'. But you might get 'I'd love it if you'd reach out to me more... I get pretty lonely and you're the only person who truly sees me. Sometimes I don't have the confidence to ask you for help.'

Now let's look at romantic relationships, because this is where it can get really tricky.

You're bumbling along, several years into a relationship. You both do your own washing, cooking and cleaning because it's just what you agreed on and it works for you both. You split the bills in half and feel good about that, you've got a healthy state of independence within the relationship itself. You feel you communicate well, but bicker from time to time as everyone does.

And then you ask the question... "What do you expect from a girlfriend? What does the ideal relationship role look like for you?"

And they come out with this: "Well... ideally I'd like to come home to a cooked meal and washed clothes, I don't think that's asking much. No nagging, just being supportive and listening when I need it. And I'd like my role to be providing enough money for you, as my partner, to be happy. I'd also like to feel needed in the relationship."

You feel your jaw drop, and an inner rage bubbling up within at the mere suggestion of you becoming a housewife. 'MISOGYNIST!' your inner voice cries... Everything you thought you knew about that person shatters in a sentence. You question everything.

But first, before you even ask that question, you must know what role *you* expect them to play, and what role you expect *yourself* to play, within a relationship.

You may feel that your role in a relationship should be to remain financially independent. You may feel that your role in a relationship should be to be able to emotionally support the other whenever they need it. Or perhaps it's providing? Perhaps it's nurturing, caregiving, organising, controlling – taking the stress away. You may expect your partner to do half the housework and nothing less. You may expect your partner to tend to the physical repairs of the home and garden (structural safety). You may expect a partner to do the driving, to book the trips and plan the holidays. Or perhaps you expect them to take care of the kids?

You have to get pretty real and pretty honest with this one. Because chances are, you've got very different expectations of each other's roles here. And creating a new 'relationship contract' isn't quite as easy when you live with someone and have spent most of your relationship running things a certain way under a false illusion.

My best advice? Devote some serious talking time to this topic. Get to the bottom of both of your belief systems. Are those beliefs how you as your soul self truly feels, or are they societal beliefs that you have absorbed? What relationships were you modelled as a child, what were the roles there? Was there ever a time you felt differently to this? Why? What happened? How did your upbringing influence the way you feel about relationships now? *Do you think this is normal, and healthy?*

Look for wiggle room. What role behaviours would you be willing to compromise on and which ones are unmoveable? Is there a way you could create new roles together that suited you as a couple better? Are there changes you could both make to allow the relationship to sit more comfortably? Are their elements of each of your belief systems that are a little outdated? Or do you need to be with someone who is better able to play the role you are looking for?

I know what you're thinking – if there's nothing wrong, why change it? Belief systems are just belief systems, we shouldn't have to change ourselves just because somebody else is stubborn.

The roles we expect each other to play will end up being the root cause of resentment and bitterness if they are not addressed and managed appropriately. Relationship roles are this invisible secret world that no one talks about until the big blowout at the end where you breakup because you never knew they were looking for you to help out around the house more because it was never communicated, but now there's too much bitterness to see past it anyway.

What do you need from me? What do you expect from me as your partner? How could I make this relationship work more smoothly? Are all great questions to ask.

'I love it when you snuggle up with me after work, it makes me feel safe and supported.'

'If you were able to help out a little more with the bills, I would appreciate it so much.'

'I'd love it if you could communicate with me when you need some space so that I can respect that.'

So, what's your role? (And where is there some room for learning?).

PART 6: HABITS

Throughout the process of writing this book, I've rediscovered the backpack of tools I had been given by life and all its ups and downs in order to share them with you, and also with me.

I had been waiting a long time to write this book, and for it to call me in some of my darkest hours took me by surprise. I honestly believed there was no way I could possibly be in a better place by the time this book was finished. I thought I'd be a fraud, selling my secrets to navigating life when they weren't even working for me. But I was wrong. The book called me exactly when it was supposed to, and found me exactly when I needed it.

Finding a place to collate all my lessons, and be able to share those – that is my greatest success. That is all I need from this world. For it to mean something more than me. And for that I will forever be grateful.

Writing this book has shown me so much about myself. That writing will forever be my calling, regardless as to whether it's seen by my eyes only, or the worlds. That I already know what I need to do, and all the answers are within if I listen carefully enough. That surrendering to the process of life, love, loss and learning is the most freeing choice you can make. And that above all, there is always, always, love.

This final section contains some of the habits you can top yourself up with to maintain a stable soul. I expect you and I have far more to learn still, and I'm so excited for that, aren't you?

Trust yourself enough to find the right ways for you. Trust yourself enough to listen to the subtle signals of the universe guiding you to where you need to be. Remind yourself, every five minutes if you need to, that you've conquered incredible things all by yourself, and that you can do it again. Remind yourself that you are already changing the world just by being you, and that every decision, every failure, every regret, has always led you to where you need to be. You will always find your way home.

Write yourself love letters, take life less seriously (but embrace the beautiful tragedies that come with it in all the intensity they desire as well), and remind yourself that everything around you is Disneyland – colourful, magical, impossible and with a high potential for fun. Never let that go.

Believe in yourself more than anybody else possibly could. Get therapy, just because. Sing in the car, just because. Take up a quirky hobby, just because. Make internet friends, just because. Trust. Just because.

There is so, so much more out there waiting for you. I honour you for being here. I adore you for choosing growth, healing, change, chance.

And if you still need to find The Will To Live, it's out there, waiting to be found. Don't give up

LESSON 34: LAZINESS IS A MYTH

'Lazy' is one of my least favourite words. I don't actually think the word should exist. I don't think it's a real thing. If somebody calls someone lazy, I immediately raise my eyebrows in the hope it pulls my skin so tight my mouth won't open and start a fight with an innocent bystander. It's not fair on them, they don't know...

It is here that I should add that I'm about as ADHD as you can get. (I can go weeks without writing this book and then BAM 7000 words in a day, for three days). Being neurodivergent means I have spent my whole life being called 'lazy'.

She can't work a normal 9-5 like everyone else: lazy.

The house is always messy even though she always seems to be cleaning it: lazy.

She can't complete assignments at the same pace as everyone else: lazy.

She hasn't been studying: lazy.

She didn't walk the dog for two days but took them out for a 10 mile walk the day before: lazy.

She lives in financial stress rather than just working more and earning more: lazy.

I could go on, and on, and on. Of the many strange medical acronyms

I have after my name (rather than Rebecca Wild PhD, it's Rebecca Wild PCOS, ADHD, Endo, EDS and so on), ADHD has been the one that's given me the most relief. I still get called lazy, but now it doesn't hurt so much. (Oh, and by the way, lazy isn't limited to neurodivergents, I just have a fair experience of how misused and misunderstood 'laziness' is).

Instead of studying, I'd be staring at the wall, infuriated that I couldn't just sit there and read the book. Instead of tidying, I'd be deep cleaning the shower drain or re-sealing the bath rather than doing the jobs I was actually meant to be doing. I'd be up until 2am every night trying to complete the assignments others had done in a day.

That wasn't laziness, that was overwhelm.

Now let's check in with Dave, the digger driver. Dave doesn't work half as hard as everyone else on site. Dave spends most of the day watching TikTok's on his phone. Dave, is lazy.

But let's look a little deeper. What if Dave isn't lazy, but unfulfilled? And so overwhelmed with the unfulfillment in his life that he has no energy left to give to it. What if Dave isn't lazy, but lacks confidence, and the fear of not being good enough consumes him so intensely that he doesn't want to try in case even his best efforts aren't enough? What if Dave isn't lazy, but battling years of unhealed trauma that plagues his mind and need constant distraction.

Maybe I'm just making excuses for people, but maybe, just maybe, I'm not...

Why wouldn't you want to do a good job at the work you do?

Because of a LACK. Because you're not paid enough, or respected enough, or valued enough.

Why wouldn't you want to give your all to projects that made a difference? That benefited others and made you feel great once they're done?

Because the negatives outweigh the positives. Because you literally don't have any capacity left to give.

Why would you not want the best for yourself? Think about it. Laziness doesn't even make sense.

Overwhelm on the other hand does make sense, and is very real, and very often ignored until burnout and breakdown. So perhaps rather than calling ourselves lazy we should start asking ourselves what's going on inside. Perhaps instead of berating ourselves for not hustling, for watching TV instead of starting a second business, we should check in with our capacity meter, and see how deep the damage runs.

Maybe it's just a few weeks of taking on more than we can manage. Or maybe it's a lifetime of overwhelm and unhealed trauma. Maybe finding where to start IS the overwhelming part. Maybe we need to change "Why am I so lazy?" to 'Why does my body need so much rest right now?".

Laziness is simply your body signalling that it needs a break to rest, or to reevaluate. And it's a signal that has become 'bad' and 'unproductive' in the modern day 'work until it breaks you' mindset, rather than a real human feeling and an intuitive and natural primal instinct.

And if we've learnt anything about hustle culture, it's that it isn't exactly 'Team Mental Health'. Intuition on the other hand, listening to our body and honouring its true needs... now we're talking.

The lesson here is to question everything, just enough. Is to question the hard-set beliefs you've had ingrained into you. To question your own bias's, judgements and the things you feel 100% about.

Because everything isn't always as it seems.

And you're not friggin lazy. You're just overwhelmed.

(Are you overwhelmed or are you just giving too much energy to things you don't care about enough?)

Be gentle with yourself.

LESSON 35: THERE ARE NO COINCIDENCES

This is one of my favourite and most magical concepts. When you start seeing everything that happens in your life as a message, everything begins to feel sacred. And when everything begins to feel sacred, life has meaning, and excitement and purpose.

The great thing about this concept too, is that it will perform its best moments when you need them the most. It will jump out at you and make you walk back to your car with a big grin on your face shaking your head in disbelief.

When you start to see everything as a lesson and everyone as a teacher, regardless of whether it feels good and easy or painful and hard, life feels a little less mean. Give it purpose. Rather than looking for a reason for suffering, find meaning within it.

Connect all the dots. 'Well, if this hadn't happened then I wouldn't have met them and wouldn't have learnt this'.

Lessons repeating themselves in an almost identical way? – I still have something to learn here.

The exact same conflict coming up in a different but healthy relationship? – What is blocking me from healing this wound?

A bizarre traffic delay happening at the worst possible time? – What opportunity is this creating for me?

When I am behind a slow driver, I continuously remind myself that this delay is for a reason. Because of this delay, I'll end up having a conversation with someone I wouldn't have had without it. Or, it will help me avoid an accident.

Everything is sacred and nothing is just 'a coincidence'. You wouldn't be the person you are today without every single experience you have been through so far, as harsh and challenging as that has been.

Some people call this way of thinking 'spiritual bypassing' and 'neglecting the opportunity to properly grieve', and that is fair enough. This is my way of thinking; it is extremely cathartic for me and has helped and healed me so much through so much of my life. It does not have to be that way for you. There does not have to be a reason. It can just be shit. That's okay. It can just be an inconvenient traffic delay, that's okay. But for me it just injects a little magic into my life, and it helps push me through.

Oftentimes these coincidences are subtle, the way you'd only notice if you were listening.

Other times they are blaringly obvious. Like the way a handyman shows up at your house to do some work after you've been through a tough time, and the first thing he says is 'Wow, you have a good energy". You laugh out loud as the universe acts as subtle as a brick, connecting you with rare like-minded individuals and a metaphysical and enlightening conversation ensues.

Or the time you get lost on the backroads, and the internet isn't working, and it starts to rain, and you end up stumbling across a Nepalese sound healing centre, where the founder just so happens to be on site for the first time in months and ends up giving you a talk on all things sound healing.

Or the way you find a sticker that says '39', so you glue it to your nails because you're a bit strange and you see it every day and wonder if it means something. A few weeks later, you start planning to write a book, and realise you've created 39 chapters, just like the number on your nails. You think nothing of it. Until you reach your final few chapters, many months later, and casually look up what the number 39 means, only to find out it is associated with spiritual and divine teachings and enlightenment, and it makes you cry.

There are clues everywhere if you look closely enough. To guide you, to reassure you, to help you have faith and find the way forward.

Just think about all the things that wouldn't have happened if you hadn't been at that place at that time, and what that would have meant for your life now.

I know sometimes life can feel cruel, vicious even, I know finding a lesson in extreme trauma isn't always beneficial. But it can be helpful in healing should you let it be – should that work for you.

Trust, surrender, and remember how much love there is out there just waiting for you. Those hidden messages, conversations that seem mystically linked to something that's been on your mind recently and insights are all there to help with your soul's journey. (There's a whole pit crew looking out for you up there, rooting for you, cheering you on. They've got posters of you in their office. Superfans I'm telling you.)

Nothing is a coincidence, including you being right here, right now.

Take what you need.

TRUST THE PROCESS

LESSON 36: ENERGY RITUALS

Rituals are an important and under-utilised part of life that help us both through everyday experiences and through tougher times. Rituals can be unique to you, or something you do as a family or group. One of my working day rituals is changing the genre of music that I'm playing when my working day is up. Doing this routinely has taught my brain that it can do it's best to close the busy work thoughts once that music comes on. Particularly if it's been a more challenging day.

What does that have to do with 'energy'? Nothing if you don't want it to. But it can also mean channelling a different kind of energy. It can mean separating negative energy of the day, or people you have been around, or places that don't light you up, and instead bringing in a more peaceful and positive energy. You can use these rituals as self-cleansing practices if that sits right for you.

A great one is changing your clothes after visiting challenging family members, it's a way of signalling to your body that you're over it, you've let it go, clean cut, just like that. You're laying a fresh new energy canvas, simply with a change of clothes. Change your clothes, change your energy.

Maybe you reward yourself with a certain treat on a Friday after work and it helps your body know you've got the weekend off. Maybe you have a certain affirmation you say every morning. Maybe you journal (gahhh journalling is a great ritual), or pull tarot with the full moon, or write yourself a love letter every Wednesday, or buy yourself flowers with your food shop.

Rituals can be great big things too — like changing your name to something that honours who you are better. Or throwing a break-up party. Or getting a tattoo you can always see that reminds you to come back to yourself. Maybe you plant a tree for a loved one who has passed, or burn things that no longer serve you (and have dodgy energy?).

Or they can be as simple and small as saving business cards from places you've visited and keeping them in a box. As making a wish when you blow the dandelion seeds into the wind in May. As whipping sage around the house or lighting a candle when the energy feels heavy there.

They key difference about rituals and everyday activities is that rituals are intentional acts of self-love and recognition. They are a clear indication you are listening to your body's signals and the way your energy works. You are responding to your energetic needs. And that isn't an easy feat, or something that comes naturally to many people.

And if you don't have rituals yet, why not pick one from above, and use it on a clear transitory moment (like after visiting difficult family) to begin to register the way your energy works.

Devote yourself to creating a magical life with everything you do.

LESSON 37: IF IT'S MEANT TO BE IN YOUR LIFE, IT WILL BE.

This is not the same as 'If he wanted to, he would' - because for reference, with the state of confidence lack and poor mental health rates across the globe, I think he could want to, but be too terrified/full of self-hatred to. This is not the same as that...

This concept is for those of us who panic about 'The Plan'. This is for my anxiety babes and my control issue babes and my existential crisis babes. It's about trusting that the Universe got your back. It's about trusting that you will always find your way home. It's about trusting yourself and your life path enough to let go. It's about a solid belief that life wants to work with your best interests at heart, even if that doesn't look the way you expected it to.

And this isn't to say you can sit on the sofa and watch Friends back-to-back for the rest of your life because you trust you're going to be a millionaire and therefore it will just show up in your pizza delivery one day.

This concept is to say that if you honour your truths, honour your feelings, honour your dreams and find a way to work with as much inner and outer harmony as possible, then everything will fall into place just as it's meant to be.

The 'one who got away' was never really for you if they didn't come back.

The interview you didn't get was just creating space for something else to come in.

The house purchase that fell through was just guiding you to a place that was going to gift you greater lessons.

If it's meant to be in your life, it will be.

The lessons you need to learn here will show up, regardless of how many times you try and stop or change them. The patterns will keep repeating themselves until you learn what you need to learn from them. No matter how much you can try and manipulate and mould a situation to work out just as you'd like it to, if it's not meant to be in your life, it won't be.

Regret can have a hold over us in a cruel way. Missed opportunities, lost moments, words you wish you'd said. Sometimes the learning is simply 'not to do it again'. But other times, the learning comes through subtle movements and unexpected pieces and cogs that are turning behind the veil.

The 'one who got away' in my life came back, years later, and showed me how to love someone.

Dropping out of university landed me in jobs that humbled me and taught me unique life skills that I may never have had the chance to learn had I stayed in the same career all my life.

Having womb surgeries and reproductive health issues led me to womb work, energy healing and an entirely different connection to what it means to bleed, that I may have just ignored had it not been such a blazing sore point in my life.

Of course, all of these lessons were meant for me in this life, but the way they appeared was nothing like the way I would have expected. It's hard when things don't go to plan when control and planning feels like safety to some of us. Surrendering to that requires immense courage and trust that doesn't come naturally.

It's a baby steps job this one. It's a meditate on it kinda thing. A write it in your affirmations journal until it sticks type of habit. And you'll have waves of being better at it than other times. It's not a linear process, but sometimes erratic and irregular.

But what it will give you is an ability to be in the present, and a willingness to surrender your soul to the greater good that feels far safer than control and planning ever did.

Life feels a lot easier when you trust, and believe, that you are going to be alright.

LESSON 38: LET'S ALL CRY ABOUT IT

Let me tell you one surefire way I know that you and I won't get on. You'll say things like:

"We don't talk about feelings in this family, that's not how we do things."

"Crying is a sign of weakness and I won't stand for it."

"The important thing is to carry on as normal, we cannot let this affect us."

As much as these three statements are nothing to do with me and simply the way you have been wired and programmed to visualise the world, it is the unwillingness to change that is problematic for me. It is the unwillingness to accept the FACT that multiple studies have shown that talking about our problems and sharing our negative emotions with another can reduce stress, strengthen our immune system, and reduce physical and emotional distress[xxviii].

Or the complete ignoration of the multiple studies showing how beneficial crying is for the body, and how it activates the parasympathetic nervous system (allowing the body to feel calm, rest and digest), releases endorphins, dulls pain, restores emotional balance and makes you happier[xxix].

Or what about the way emotional tears have an entirely different composition to tears produced when chopping an onion for example, containing more protein-based hormones, meaning they travel down the face more slowly and are more visible to others? A neurobiological process theorised to be used to rally support and encourage social bonding[xxx]. It is something uniquely present in human beings, almost like crying is a necessary process (even in adulthood) of social bonding and emotional processing.

I quite literally want to bang my head against the wall when I hear people slut-shaming big feelings and tears. Not only does it generate a toxic, restrictive and inhuman environment, but it creates a layer of fear and shame behind completely natural behaviours that are purely there to make you feel better and navigate the tough stuff. It would be like criticising someone for going for a pee. It's bananas.

Our feelings are simply messengers alerting you to an emotional process that needs some working through. Tears are bloody brilliant ways to do that. They aren't bad, or weak. They represent a liberation of emotion through your body. The movement and release of withheld energy and feeling.

I have cried after sex. Both in joy and in grief. I have cried after watching those damn animal rescue videos on TikTok, sometimes repeatedly in a day when it keeps coming back to mind. I have cried after tasting food so good I thought I might explode. I have cried after tripping so hard I felt all the love in the whole wide world in the palm of my hand. I have cried after being told 'I love you', both in panic and in ecstasy. I have cried in grief, oh I have cried in grief. I have sobbed, wailed, wept, whined, screamed, howled, roared with tears that wanted letting go of. I have cried and to date, it hasn't killed me.

I have cried and it hasn't made me any less of a woman, a business owner, an artist, a lover.

Men will cry and (despite the belief of some radicalistic internet gurus that could do with a good dose of therapy) their penis's will not fall off. It will not make them any less of a man, a father, a leader or provider.

I want us to get to a point where someone cries or someone talks about sad things, and rather than mass panic and 'are you okay!?'s and panicked 'hope things get better soon!'s ensuing, there is simply calm. There is simply acknowledgment. There is simply 'ah, healing, feeling, being. I love it. Good for you.'

It's great to have people look out for us, I'm not knocking that. I just seek a day where emotions aren't seen as bad and frightening and concerning – just emotions. Beautiful, necessary, important and also just passing by.

So please, let's all cry about it. Let's have a crying party and move through shit together. Let's witness our complete and utter humanness, our primal selves using our primal mechanisms the way they were intended. Let us bond in pain and bond in love and bond in feeling. Let us guide each other through with compassion and gratitude and pride for one another. Let us lift each other up (but only when we are ready).

Let's all cry about it.

LESSON 39: THE OPPOSITE OF TRAUMA IS PLAY (AND OTHER USEFUL LIFE TIPS)

This isn't the kind of self-help book where I give you lots of basic bitch advice based on research studies and internet trends, but for the sake of all thing's mental health and the outrageous assumption that one of you out there doesn't have social media, I shall briefly address the following suggestions.

1. Eat Better. Whatever that means to you. Explore and try everything to see what feels right for your body (not just what it says on your favourite influencers account). 'Better' for me, as someone with a history of eating disorders, will mean something completely different to what 'better' means for you, and that's okay.

2. Stretch. Or Yoga. Or intuitive dance. Or 'cooling down at the gym'. Or whatever your ego feels safe to call it, I don't care, just try it. Listen to it. Ask your body what it needs and let it respond how it wants to. Trust that it will show you the way to releasing tension should you just give it the chance to speak up. There is shit you are holding that can be moved through movement, trust me on that one.

3. Get outside or get your face in the sun. Some people say it has to be before 10am[xxxi] to help you sleep better. Some people say you should sun your buttholes to receive divine messages from spirit. All I know for sure is that natural light makes us feel

better, even if you're only getting it for five minutes (it's still five minutes, go you).

4. Find people you can play with (not like that...). The opposite of trauma is play, it's how we regulate ourselves as children and how we process challenging ideas and concepts presented to us. We stop playing as adults because it's not 'cool' anymore. Until you find someone who doesn't care about being cool and will play with you. Who will having a splashing match with you in the ocean or a pool or bath. Who will chase you round a supermarket laughing hysterically because you stole their shoe. Who will play games involving storytelling and wild imaginations. I want you to find laughter wherever you are. Alone or with company. It's always there, hiding, waiting to be found.

5. Play with yourself (absolutely like that). Self-pleasure is maybe the most underrated mood-boosting tool to exist. Is it shame? Is it a lack of awareness? Is it time and privacy? I could write a book on it. If this isn't part of your weekly selfcare ritual (at least) then I strongly suggest giving it a go. And it doesn't have to be all fingers and thumbs and rubber rods and vibrating things like porn says it should be. There are so, so many other ways, and ways that are more suited for you. Get experimenting!

6. See a doctor and get your bloods done. This one is boring but I'm a hypochondriac so wouldn't be truly authentic if I didn't include it. As much as my inner hippie despises western medicine, I also have chronic health conditions that directly affect my mood, hormone regulation, food and vitamin absorption (including the ones that make you happy) and general mental health. There *could* be something going on in your body that is affecting your mood, and as a data nerd, it's fun to have your blood test results anyway. Stick them on your fridge or something.

7. Get therapy. This is a super privileged thing to say from

someone whose mum has paid for her therapy during the many years of health-related financial struggles I have ensued. But if it is an option for you, take it. We cannot do this world alone. We should not do this pain alone. And if a 'therapist' is too embarrassing for you, call them a 'coach' instead. For the majority of us who cannot afford therapy ourselves, there are free resources and charities who can provided some services, and secondly, there is a host of free information online that can be a great place to start. Buy or borrow books written by therapists, and by people who have been through hard shit and survived. Study yourself like an A level English essay. Take notes on your behaviours, attitudes, thoughts. Journal. Make video diaries. Do weekly and monthly reflections. Notice the ways you are changing and growing. Notice it all (but don't fixate so much that you get entirely lost inside your head and then become obsessive and depressive like I did).

Stay curious. Stay learning. Stay open-minded to your own changes.

I'm right in that boat with you too.

"A friend took me to the most amazing place the other day. It's called the Augusteum. Octavian Augustus built it to house his remains. When the barbarians came they trashed it a long with everything else. The great Augustus, Rome's first true great emperor. How could he have imagined that Rome, the whole world as far as he was concerned, would be in ruins. It's one of the quietest, loneliest places in Rome. The city has grown up around it over the centuries. It feels like a precious wound, a heartbreak you won't let go of because it hurts too good. We all want things to stay the same. Settle for living in misery because we're afraid of change, of things crumbling to ruins. Then I looked at around to this place, at the chaos it has endured - the way it has been adapted, burned, pillaged and found a way to build itself back up again. And I was reassured, maybe my life hasn't been so chaotic, it's just the world that is, and the real trap is getting attached to any of it. Ruin is a gift. Ruin is the road to transformation."

— Elizabeth Gilbert, Eat, Pray, Love

A Little Thank You

To my friends and family for always egging me on, being my cheerleaders, and having enormous patience with me throughout this process. You've *almost* stopped asking me when the book will be released, and I've *almost* stopped answering 'the timing is as it is meant to be, it's all relevant!'.

To my partner and my gorgeous soul dog, for showing me love and joy in every day. I feel so blessed to have been granted these experiences with you both, for as long as I get them.

To my online community for giving me space to share my inner thoughts, and a vision to dream bigger. The way you accept me as I am lights me up.

And to life, for the pain, the suffering, the love and the learning. What a ride this has been.

---

[i] There's a name for this – passive suicidality. See your doctor. :)

[ii] Jung, C.G. (2014). *The Archetypes and the Collective Unconscious.*

[iii] Cohen, K.S., 1999. The way of qigong: The art and science of Chinese energy healing.

[iv] I believe this means 'wild party', but I can't be sure. Trying to be down with the kids.

[v] Marsland et al, 2006 – Happiness and infection

[vi] Carstensen et al (2011) - Happiness and Life Expectancy

[vii] Bhattacharyya, Whitehead, Rakhit & Steptoe (2008) - Happiness and heart health

[viii] Dubois et al (2012) – Happiness and Eating Healthier

[ix] Sonja Lyubomirsky, Laura King, Ed Diener (2005) - Does Happiness lead to success?

[x] I highly recommend reading Janina Fishers informative book "Healing the Fragmented Selves of Trauma Survivors: Overcoming Internal Self-Alienation" for a better understanding of human stress responses.

[xi] Schedlowski, M. and Schmidt, R.E. (1996). Stress und Immunsystem.

[xii] Schedlowski, M. and Schmidt, R.E. (1996). Stress und Immunsystem.

[xiii] Another book recommendation! The Body Keeps the Score by Bessel Van Der Kolk explores links between emotional trauma and physical health. It is a pretty gobsmacking read, and very worth it.

[xiv] Holt-Lunstad J, Smith TB, Layton JB, 2010, Social relationships and mortality risk: a meta-analytic review. PLoS Med.

[xv] Liebschutz J, Savetsky JB, Saitz R, Horton NJ, Lloyd-Travaglini C, Samet JH, 2002, The relationship between sexual and physical abuse and substance abuse consequences. J Subst Abuse Treat.

[xvi] Fisher, J. (2017) Healing the fragmented selves of trauma survivors: Overcoming internal self-alienation. New York: Routledge.

[xvii] Appleton J, 2018, The Gut-Brain Axis: Influence of Microbiota on Mood and Mental Health. Integr Med (Encinitas).

[xviii] https://www.ncbi.nlm.nih.gov/pmc/articles/PMC8201496/

[xix] Amawi, R.M.; Murdoch, M.J, 2022, Understanding Color Associations and Their Effects on Expectations of Drugs' Efficacies. *Pharmacy*.

[xx] University of Liverpool, 2008, "Contraceptive Pill Influences Partner Choice." ScienceDaily.

[xxi] Bertram, S. M., Loranger, M. J., Thomson, I. R., Harrison, S. J., Ferguson, G. L., Reifer, M. L.Gowaty, P. A., 2016, Linking mating preferences to sexually selected traits and offspring viability: good versus complementary genes hypotheses. *Animal Behavior, 119*, 75-86.

[xxii] Earp BD, Wudarczyk OA, Foddy B, Savulescu J, 2017, Addicted to love: What is love addiction and when should it be treated? Philos Psychiatr Psychol.

[xxiii] S. Zeki, 2007, The neurobiology of love, FEBS Letters, Volume 581, Issue 14.

[xxiv] Levinson, D, 1986, *American Psychologist*, Vol 41(1), 3-13.

[xxv] Chapman, Gary D, 2010, The Five Love Languages. Walker Large Print.

[xxvi] Raitasalo, K., Holmila, M., Jääskeläinen, M., & Santalahti, P. (2019). The effect of the severity of parental alcohol abuse on mental and behavioural disorders in children. European child & adolescent psychiatry, 28(7), 913–922.

[xxvii] Sandra E. Black & Erik Grönqvist & Björn Öckert, 2018. "Born to Lead? The Effect of Birth Order on Noncognitive Abilities," The Review of Economics and Statistics, MIT Press, vol. 100(2), pages 274-286

[xxviii] Pennebaker, Kiecolt-Glaser, & Glaser, 1988.

[xxix] Gračanin A, Bylsma LM, Vingerhoets AJ, 2014, Is crying a self-soothing behavior? Front Psychol.

[xxx] Bylsma LM, Gračanin A, Vingerhoets AJJM, 2019, The neurobiology of human crying. Clin Auton Res.

[xxxi] Holth JK, Fritschi SK, Wang C, et al, 2019, The sleep-wake cycle regulates brain interstitial fluid tau in mice and CSF tau in humans. *Science*.

Printed in Great Britain
by Amazon

40474842R00111